THE DAYLIGHT MOON

THE DAYLIGHT MOON

Poems by Les A. Murray

CARCANET

First published in Australia in 1987
by Angus & Robertson Publishers

First published in Great Britain in 1988 by
Carcanet Press Limited
208-212 Corn Exchange Buildings
Manchester M4 3BQ

British Library Cataloguing in Publication Data
    Murray, Les A.
        The Daylight Moon.
        I. Title
        821   PR9619.3.M76/

        ISBN 0 85635 779 0

The publisher acknowledges financial assistance from the
Arts Council of Great Britain

Printed in England by SRP Ltd, Exeter

To the glory of God

Acknowledgements

Poems in this book have been published in the *Adelaide Review, Age Monthly Review, Agenda, American Poetry Review, Antipodes, Atlantic Monthly, Australian, Cambridge Review, Catholic Weekly, Civil Liberty, Collins Dove Anthology of Australian Religious Verse, Hermes, Island, Little Magazine* (New York), Mattara Prize Anthology *An Inflection of Silence* 1986, *New York Review of Books, Northern Perspective, Overland, Planet, PN Review, Poetry Australia, Poetry Canada Review, Poetry Ireland, Pol Arts Review, Quadrant, Sydney Morning Herald, Scripsi, Simply Living, Sud, Threepenny Review, 2 + 2, Times Literary Supplement* and *Verse* (Oxford), and some have been broadcast by the Australian Broadcasting Corporation, the British Broadcasting Corporation, Radio 2GB and stations 2SER-FM and 2BOB-FM.

I am grateful to the Literature Board of the Australia Council, the Canadian Writers Union, Persea Books (New York), the Library of Congress, the National Library of Australia, the University of Sydney and La Trobe University for support, assistance and hospitality extended to me during the years when these poems were being written.

Contents

Flood Plains on the Coast Facing Asia

Hitching blur to a caged propeller
with its motor racket swelling
barroom to barrage, our aluminium
airboat has crossed the black coffee
lagoon and swum out onto
one enormous crinkling green.
Now like a rocket loudening
to liftoff, it erects the earsplitting
wigwam we must travel in
everywhere here, and starts skimming
at speed on the never-never
meadows of the monsoon wetland.

Birds lift, scattering before us
over the primeval irrigation,
leaf-running jacanas, twin-boomed
with supplicant bare feet for tails;
knob-headed magpie geese
row into the air ahead of us;
waterlilies lean away, to go
under as we overrun them
and resurrect behind us.
We leave at most a darker green
trace on the universal glittering
and, waterproof in cream and blue,
waterlilies on their stems, circling.

Our shattering car
crossing exposed and seeping spaces
brings us to finely stinking places,
yet whatever riceless paddies
we reach, of whatever grass
there is always sheeting spray
underhull for our passage;
and the Intermediate Egret leaps
aloft out of stagnant colours
and many a double-barrelled crossbow
shoots vegetable breath emphatically
from the haunts of flaking buffalo;
water glinting everywhere, like ice,
we traverse speeds humans once reached
in such surroundings mainly
as soldiers, in the tropic wars.

At times, we fold our windtunnel
away, in its blackened steel sail

and sit, for talk and contemplation.
For instance, off the deadly islet,
a swamp-surrounded sandstone knoll
split, cabled, commissured
with fig trees' python roots.
Watched by distant plateau cliffs
stitched millennially in every crevice
with the bark-entubed dead
we do not go ashore.
Those hills are ancient stone gods
just beginning to be literature.

We release again the warring sound
of our peaceful tour, and go sledding
headlong through mounded paperbark
copses, on reaches of maroon
grit, our wake unravelling
over green curd where logs lie digesting
and over the breast-lifting deeps
of the file snake, whom the women here
tread on, scoop up, clamp head-first in their teeth
and jerk to death, then carry home as meat.

Loudest without speech, we shear
for miles on the paddock of nymphaeas
still hoisting up the paired pied geese,
their black goslings toddling below them.
We, a family with baby and two friends
one swift metal skin above the food-chains,
the extensible wet life-chains of which
our civility and wake are one stretch,
the pelicans circling over us another
and the cat-napping peace of the secure,
of eagles, lions and two-year-old George
asleep beneath his pink linen hat as
we enter domains of flowering lotus.

In our propeller's stiffened silence
we stand up among scalloped leaves
that are flickering for hundreds of acres
on their deeper water. The lotus
prove a breezy nonhuman gathering
of this planet, with their olive-studded
rubbery cocktail glasses, loose carmine roses,
salmon buds like the five-fingertips-joined
gesture of summation, of *ecco!*
waist-high around us in all their greenery
on yeasty frog water. We receive this
sidelong, speaking our wiry language
in which so many others ghost and flicker.

We discuss Leichhardt's party and their qualities
when, hauling the year 1845
through here, with spearheads embedded in it,
their bullock drays reached and began skirting
this bar of literal water
after the desert months which had been
themselves a kind of swimming,
a salt undersea plodding, monster-haunted
with odd very pure surfacings.
We also receive, in drifts of calm
hushing, which fret the baby boy,
how the fuzzed gold innumerable cables
by which this garden hangs skyward
branch beneath the surface, like dreams.

The powerful dream of being harmless,
the many chains snapped and stretched hard for that:
both shimmer behind our run back
toward the escarpments where stallion-eyed
Lightning lives, who'd shiver all heights
down and make of the earth
one oozing, feeding peneplain.
Unprotected Lightning: there are his wild horses
and brolgas, and far heron not rising.
Suddenly we run over a crocodile.
On an unlilied deep, bare even
of minute water fern, it leaped out,
surged man-swift straight under us. We ran over it.
We circle back. Unhurt, it floats, peering
from each small eye turret, then annuls
buoyancy and merges subtly under,
swollen leathers becoming gargoyle stone,
chains of contour, with pineapple abdomen.

Cumulus

Repeatedly out of grazed plateaux, the Dividing
Range assumes, soaring after gliding,
into high countries, not peaked but cumulus
in evergreen black and mossy bleached khaki
out under antarctic grey and razory blues,
horizons above the nation, now visited rarely
except in polemic hiking, or on the ski niveaux.
We turned away to ochre and surf sands long ago
and secret cattleyards never formed a traceable city.

White cloud still assembles daily along each island
far above our South Sea levels. Mist forest, tussock sops
under redoubled height drink fog along the Tops
and newly-earthed rivers edge out of sphagnum overloads
to shin down human clay and unhuman cobbled roads
to the short east, to the brown west ocean of land;
the cello necks of tree ferns spread as they come uncurled
and screech-red parrots fly, with many stops
toward the beech trees of the southern world.

On the varying heights where stupendous heights are brewed
out of clear air by pitch and altitude
few have yet lived, in all the centuries. Some have stayed.
Many themes attended the hibernation of Ned Kelly:
the fat moth-feast of the tribes, whip bird and rifle bird,
moleskin prospectors each working his vein of solitude;
Thunderbolt emerging from the wet cave of his treasure
sights a coach down through timber, spurs into ballad measure —
but these disappear down the crumples of the possum-skin rug,

the great ravines of catchment. Jindabygone, Adamemory.
Of Governors fleeing heat on the hill stations, we recall Jimmy,
but the sleepout in the dark ranges has weakened its tug
and retreat is continually modelled. Our plateau capital
avoids its own heights and nearby mountains. They are all
cloud-shadowed with new dry forest. The vixen feeds her cubs,
and kangaroos fold down to graze, above the human suburbs.
Neither fantasy nor fear has built an eagle's nest fortress
to top our nonfiction poetry. We've put the wild above us.

Federation Style on the Northern Rivers

And entering on the only smooth road
this steamer glides past the rattling shipyard
where they're having the usual Aboriginal
whale-feast in reverse, with scaffolding and planking;
engine smoke marching through blue sheoak trees
along the edge of Jack Robertson farms,
the river opens and continually opens

and lashed on deck, a Vauxhall car
intricate in brass, with bonnet grooves,
a bulb to squawk, great guillotine levers,
high diamond-buttoned leather club chairs
and dressing-table windscreen to flash afar:
in British cherry metal, detailed in mustard
it cruises up country with a moveless wheel.

In the town it approaches, a Habsburg-yellow store
Provisions — Novelties — J. Cornwell Prop.
contains a knot of debt that has reached
straining point, tugging between many poor
selector farmers and several not necessarily
rich city suppliers. Mobilised, it can tear
the store apart, uproot many families

and tomorrow the auditor will be in town
and the car will be parked just where he comes
after a prolonged hilarious midday dinner
I see your town's acquired a motor —
You fancy those beasts, do you, Stickney?
One face grows inspired, in step with the other.
What is that sly joker Cornwell at?

asks the Bank of Australasia's swank bow window:
How can he have afforded a motor?
but a schooner bee deflects the questioner.
Would you like to take a spin in her,
Stickney? — I daresay your books will wait
*for half an hour...*One mounts from the left,
one hoists the crankhandle. Directly, indirectly

they wind down the street over horsemanures
of varying fatness, past the Coffee Palace
unconcerned with ales — *Stickney, you're a marvel!*
Just aim her straight and don't shout Whoa!
Tread on that to slow her: don't tug the wheel —
Children running, neighbours cheering, *Go it, Jim!*
Mr Cornwell lifts his hat to the faces greeting him.

Smashing water-windows along the parallel
wheeltracks of the cart-cut river road
they pass the deeply-laden Cornwell shop-boat
Turn inland here: we will have drier going.
I agree she'd be a buy, Stickney: I'd have to think —
Think how to waste more afternoon
with the tall affection of local tales:

...And old Tom Beattie managing himself
along, like a bad horse; you hear him curse it:
Hold up, you bugger! Walk! — Mr Cornwell,
we should get back, to your ledgers. — Yes.
Take the left fork two miles on. A shortcut —
The shortcut ends in blackpudding bog
and no country curricles bowling by it.

Dear God, Cornwell, I must catch tomorrow's boat!
but heaving, corduroying, pole-levering all fail
and Cornwell must vanish through the rung timber.
For Stickney there will now accrue a wait
heavy as blacksoil around buried wheels.
Shanks' pony? Not I. Not through snaky bush.
He watches a swamp pheasant's sailing flight

and on the creekbank, in a place where cattle,
the white man's firesticks, can't come
he finds a child's small bowerbird farm:
scraped roads, wharf, little twig cattleyards,
clay beasts. A new world, already immemorial.
He will tighten his coat against evening chill
long before Cornwell reappears with helpers.

That night the yellow store will burn
in a jammed eye-parching abolishment of proof
and the car, strangely spotless, will not be harmed.
Tomorrow the innocent owner will collect it.
The steamer hoots. *Cornwell, now that you're*
safely ruined: where did you go yesterday?
— I had to dodge certain bandicoot farms

where the little ones bolt up under the house
at the sight of a stranger. I've never cared
to be a stranger who threatens children.
They part, across water, with the ghost of a salute.
Certain surnames will now survive in the district.
As the town declines through the mulberry years
Cornwell will receive odd grateful sovereigns.
The rebuilt store will be kept by a Hogan.

Easter 1984

When we saw human dignity
healing humans in the middle of the day

we moved in on him slowly
under the incalculable gravity

of old freedom, of our own freedom,
under atmospheres of consequence, of justice

under which no one needs to thank anyone.
If this was God, we would get even.

And in the end we nailed him,
lashed, spittled, stretched him limb from limb

We would settle with dignity
for the anguish it had caused us,

we'd send it to be abstract again,
we would set it free.

O

But we had raised up evolution.
It would not stop being human.

Ever afterwards, the accumulation
of freedom would end in this man

whipped, bloodied, getting the treatment.
It would look like man himself getting it.

He was freeing us, painfully, of freedom,
justice, dignity — he was discharging them

of their deadly ambiguous deposit,
remaking out of them the primal day

in which he was free not to have borne it
and we were free not to have done it,

free never to torture man again,
free to believe him risen.

O

Remember the day when life increased,
explainably or outright, was haloed in poignancy,

straight life, given not attained, unlurching ecstasy,
arrest of the guards for once, and ourself released,

splendour taking detail, beyond the laughter-and-tears
if those were gateway to it, a still or moving utterness

in and all around us. Four have been this human
night and day, steadily. Three fell, two went on.

A laser of this would stand the litter-bound or Lazarus
upright, stammering, or unshroud absent Jesus

whose anguish was to be for a whole day lost to this,
making of himself the companionway of our species

up from where such love is an unreal, half-forgotten
peak, and not the baseline of the human.

Physiognomy on the Savage Manning River

Walking on that early shore, in our bodies,
the autumn ocean has become wasp-waisted:
a scraped timber mansion hung in showering
ropework is crabbing on the tide's flood,
swarming, sway, and shouting,
entering the rivermouth over the speedy bar.

As it calms into the river, the Tahitian
helmsman, a pipe-smoking archer,
draws and tightens the wheel. The spruce captain
meanwhile celebrates the bohême of revolutions
with a paper cigarette, and the carpenter,
deepwater man, combs his sulky boy's hair.

Seo abhainn mar loch — the polished river is indeed
like a loch, without flow, clear to the rainforest islands
and the Highland immigrants on deck, remarking it
keep a hand, or a foot, on their bundles and nail-kegs.
No equipment is replaceable: there's only one of anything,
experience they will hand down.

Beyond the river brush extends the deserted
Aboriginal hunting park. There is far less blue
out in the grassland khaki than in our lifetime
though the hills are darkening, sprinkling outward,
closing on crusted lagoons. Nowhere a direct line;
no willows yet, nor any houses.
Those are in the low hills upriver.
Beyond are the ranges, edge over edge, like jumbled sabres.

Crocodile chutes slant out of the riverbank forest
where great logs have been launched.
It is the feared long-unburnable
dense forest of the dooligarl. The cannibal solitary
humanoid of no tribe. Here, as worldwide, he and she
are hairy, nightmare-agile, with atavisms of the feet.
Horror can be ascribed and strange commissions given
to the fireless dooligarl. Killer, here, of gingery bat-hunters.

Tiptoeing after its slung leadline, the ship moves forward
for hours into the day. Raising the first dogleg paddocks,
the first houses, the primal blowflies.
Soup and clothing
boil in a fire-hut, in cauldrons slung on steel saws
there where next century's pelicans will haunt the Fish Cooperative.

The gossip on the river is all Miss Isabella Kelly:
triumphing home with her libel case now won
and, for her months in gaol, a thousand pounds compensation
she has found her stations devastated:
yards smashed, homestead burnt, cattle lifted
(irrecoverable nods are winked here).
Now she has sailed to England in her habitual
infuriated self esteem.
She will have Charles Dickens write her story.
Voices, calling God to forgive them, wish her drownded.

Isabella Mary Kelly. The shadowy first landholder.
Now she has given the district a larger name
to drop than her own. She, who rode beside
her walking convicts three days through the wilderness
to have them flogged half-insane in proper form
at Port Macquarie and Raymond Terrace
then walked them immediately back,
her crosshatched harem,
she who told the man who dragged her from swift floodwater
"You waste your gallantry. You are still due a lashing.
Walk on, croppy."

Isabella Kelly, of the sidesaddle acerbities,
grazier and pistol shot
throned and footless in her hooped midcentury skirts,
for some years it has been she,
and perhaps it really was she, who had the deadly crystals
mixed into scones for the natives at Belbora,
Miss Kelly all alone. The colonies' earlier Kelly.
Jilted in Dublin — or is that an acanthus leaf
of motivation, modelled over something barer?
Suddenly her time has passed.
Death in a single room in chilly Sydney
still lies ahead — and being confused with Kate Kelly —
but she has moved already into her useful legend.

Now up every side creek a youth in a cabbagetree hat
is rocking like a steersman, feinting like a boxer:
every stone of gravel must go a round or two
in a circling dish, and the pouring of waters be adjusted.
The same on every track round the heads of rivers:
men escaping the black mills
and families tired of a thousand years' dim tenancy
are entering the valley beside their jolting stacks;
there is even the odd spanker
reins in hand behind trotters, on a seat like a chocolate éclair,
though he is as yet rare;
more are riding through horse-high grass, and into timber
that thickens, like work, to meet their mighty need of it.

The ship is tied up meanwhile in a sort
of farmyard dockland:
pigs under the wharf, saddles, pumpkin patches, corn boats.
The men unloading her, who never doff their shirts
are making whips of tin;
this one who has worn the white clay girdle of the Bora,
of sung rebirth, now plies a lading hook
to keep his Kentish wife.
At spell-oh time, they will share a pipe of tobacco
which she has shaved from the succulent twist with her case-knife.

Farther upriver, men are rolling out onto their wharf
big solid barrels of a mealy wetness
and others with axes are dismembering downed cattle
in jarring sight of yarded herds. They heave the pieces
into huge smoking trypots. It is the boiling-down,
a kind of inland sealing.
The boiled-out meat is pitched down a cloacal gully.

All that can be exported of the squatters' cattle,
of the spinster Kelly's cattle and the others',
is their tallow, for candles.
Lights for the sickroom, lustre for pianoforte sconces.
Cattle distilled to a fluted wax, and sea creatures
sublimated to a liquor light the readers
of Charles Darwin and Charles Dickens.
On sleeping skins, snorting boys drip melted cattle.

Now the gently wrecking cornfields relax, and issue
parents and children. What do families offer us?
Some protection from history,
a tough school of forgiveness.
After the ship has twitched minutely out of
focus and back, as many times as there were barrels
and night has assumed the slab huts and sawn houses
the faces drinking tea by their various lights
include some we had thought modern. The mask of unappeasable
rage is there, and those of scorn's foundling aristocracy,
among the timeless sad and contented faces,
the vacant and remote faces. Only the relative
licensing of expressions is wholly different.
Blame is not yet privileged.

And, walking on that early shore in our bodies
(perhaps the only uncowardly way to do history)
if we asked leading questions, we might hear,
short of a ringing ear,
something like: We do what's to be done
and some things because we can.
Don't be taking talk out of me.

Such not only from the haughtily dreaming,
intelligent, remorseless, secretly amused still face
of Isabella Kelly.
As the Highlandman said
eating his first meal of fresh beef and cornmeal porridge
after landing today:
Thig lá choin duibh fhathast. The black dog will have his day yet.
Not every dog, as in English, but the black dog.

The Dream of Wearing Shorts Forever

To go home and wear shorts forever
in the enormous paddocks, in that warm climate,
adding a sweater when winter soaks the grass,

to camp out along the river bends
for good, wearing shorts, with a pocketknife,
a fishing line and matches,

or there where the hills are all down, below the plain,
to sit around in shorts at evening
on the plank verandah —

If the cardinal points of costume
are Robes, Tat, Rig and Scunge,
where are shorts in this compass?

They are never Robes
as other bareleg outfits have been:
the toga, the kilt, the lava-lava
the Mahatma's cotton dhoti;

archbishops and field marshals
at their ceremonies never wear shorts.
The very word
means underpants in North America.

Shorts can be Tat,
Land-Rovering bush-environmental tat,
socio-political ripped-and-metal-stapled tat,
solidarity-with-the-Third World tat tvam asi,

likewise track-and-field shorts worn to parties
and the further humid, modelling negligée
of the Kingdom of Flaunt,
that unchallenged aristocracy.

More plainly climatic, shorts
are farmers' rig, leathery with salt and bonemeal,
are sailors' and branch bankers' rig,
the crisp golfing style
of our youngest male National Costume.

Most loosely, they are Scunge,
ancient Bengal bloomers or moth-eaten hot pants
worn with a former shirt,
feet, beach sand, hair
and a paucity of signals.

Scunge, which is real negligée
housework in a swimsuit, pyjamas worn all day,
is holiday, is freedom from ambition.
Scunge makes you invisible
to the world and yourself.

The entropy of costume,
scunge can get you conquered by more vigorous cultures
and help you to notice it less.

To be or to become
is a serious question posed by a work-shorts counter
with its pressed stacks, bulk khaki and blue,
reading Yakka or King Gee, crisp with steely warehouse odour.

Satisfied ambition, defeat, true unconcern,
the wish and the knack for self-forgetfulness
all fall within the scunge ambit
wearing board shorts or similar;
it is a kind of weightlessness.

Unlike public nakedness, which in Westerners
is deeply circumstantial, relaxed as exam time,
artless and equal as the corsetry of a hussar regiment,

shorts and their plain like
are an angelic nudity,
spirituality with pockets!
A double updraft as you drop from branch to pool!

Ideal for getting served last
in shops of the temperate zone
they are also ideal for going home, into space,
into time, to farm the mind's Sabine acres
for product or subsistence.

Now that everyone who yearned to wear long pants
has essentially achieved them,
long pants, which have themselves been underwear
repeatedly, and underground more than once,
it is time perhaps to cherish the culture of shorts,

to moderate grim vigour
with the knobble of bare knees,
to cool bareknuckle feet in inland water,
slapping flies with a book on solar wind
or a patient bare hand, beneath the cadjiput trees,

to be walking meditatively
among green timber, through the grassy forest

towards a calm sea
and looking across to more of that great island
and the further topics.

At the Aquatic Carnival

Two racing boats seen from the harmonic railing
of this road bridge quit their wakes,
plane above their mirroring shield-forms
and bash the river, flat out, their hits batts of appliqué
violently spreading, their turnings eiderdown
abolishing translucency before the frieze of people,
and rolled-over water comes out to the footings of the carnival.

Even up drinking coffee-and-froth in the town
prodigious sound rams through arcades and alleyways
and burrs in our teeth, beneath the slow nacelle
of a midsummer ceiling fan.
No wonder pelicans vanish from their river at these times.
How, we wonder, does that sodden undersized one
who hangs around the Fish Co-op get by?
The pert wrymouth with the twisted upper beak.

It cannot pincer prey, or lid its lower scoop
and so lives on guts, mucking in with the others
who come and go. For it to leave would be death.
Its trouble looks like a birth defect, not an injury
and raises questions.
There are poetics would require it to be pecked
to death by fellow pelicans, or kids to smash it with a stick,
preserving a hard cosmos.

In fact it came with fellow pelicans, parents maybe
and has been around for years. Humans who feed it
are sentimental, perhaps — but what to say
of humans who refused to feed a lame bird?
Nature is not human-hearted. But it is one flesh
or we could not imagine it. And we could not eat.

Nature is not human-hearted. So the animals
come to man, at first in their extremity:
the wild scrub turkeys entering farms in drought-time,
the done fox suddenly underfoot among dog-urgers
(that frantic compliment, that prayer never granted by dogs)
or the shy birds perching on human shoulders and trucks
when the mountains are blotted out in fiery dismemberment.

Such meetings enlarge the white middle term of claim
which quivers between the dramatic red and blue poles
of fight-or-flight.
The claim exercised by pelicans
on the riverbank lawn who tap you for a sandwich

or the water-dragon in flared and fretted display
who opened its head at me, likewise for a sandwich,

by the tiny birds who materialised and sang
when my wife sang in the sleeper-cutting forest
down Stoney Creek Road. And the famous dolphins.
Today, though, men are fighting
the merciful wars of surplus, on the battered river,
making their own wide wings, and water skiers
are hoisting the inherent white banner, making it stretch
and stream both ways at once, like children's drawings
of ships or battle, out in front of the carnival.

The Sleepout

Childhood sleeps in a verandah room
in an iron bed close to the wall
where the winter over the railing
swelled the blind on its timber boom

and splinters picked lint off warm linen
and the stars were out over the hill;
then one wall of the room was forest
and all things in there were to come.

Breathings climbed up on the verandah
when dark cattle rubbed at a corner
and sometimes dim towering rain stood
for forest, and the dry cave hunched woollen.

Inside the forest was lamplit
along tracks to a starry creek bed
and beyond lay the never-fenced country,
its full billabongs all surrounded

by animals and birds, in loud crustings,
and something kept leaping up amongst them.
And out there, to kindle whenever
dark found it, hung the daylight moon.

Tropical Window

Out through a long bright window
are three headlands ruched together
on an ivory drawstring of beach. Salad and jade
over freckled pancake rock, each
is washed at foot by noonday suds intermittently
and some yachts are pinned with tall spears to the bay.

This horizontal window
is lamp and sole brilliant picture
to a shadowy cane room
where people stir instant drinks. There is the man
with sunglasses at his throat like sleek electrodes
or a very high tech bow tie
and the woman with the luminous
ruby signet of the smoker. And another
figure saying We need more passive verbs:

I am sneezed, for example (and just try to resist!) or:
You are coughed. More coughed about than coughing —
But the windowed littoral
distracts them again and again. The motionless
shellburst palms, on the skyline, over the golf course,
the sea's lucent linoleum,
the near trees with green-ants' nests
square-folded out of living leaves, like Japanese packages.

If the three stepped out
into that scene, humidity and glare would sandbag them,
make them fretful tourists.
Not coated glass but simple indoor contrast
has tuned the hyaline
to a sourceless cerebral light
and framing has made the window photo-realist,
a style of art everybody now feels they have been
in. And will be in again
at any immortal democratic moment.

Louvres

In the banana zone, in the poinciana tropics
reality is stacked on handsbreadth shelving,
open and shut, it is ruled across with lines
as in a gleaming gritty exercise book.

The world is seen through a cranked or levered
weatherboarding of explosive glass
angled floor-to-ceiling. Horizons which metre
the dazzling outdoors into green-edged couplets.

In the louvred latitudes
children fly to sleep in triplanes, and
cool nights are eerie with retracting flaps.

Their houses stand aloft among bougainvillea,
covered bridges that lead down a shining hall
from love to mystery to breakfast,
from babyhood to moving-out day

and visitors shimmer up in columnar gauges
to touch lives lived behind gauze
in a lantern of inventory,
slick vector geometries glossing the months of rain.

There, nudity is dizzily cubist, and directions
have to include: stage left, add an inch of breeze
or: enter a glistening tendril.

Every building of jinked and slatted ledges
is at times a squadron of inside-out
helicopters, humming with rotor fans.

For drinkers under cyclonic pressure, such
a house can be a bridge of scythes —
groundlings scuffing by stop only for dénouements.

But everyone comes out on platforms of command
to survey cloudy flame-trees, the plain of streets, the future:
only then descending to the level of affairs

and if these things are done in the green season
what to do in the crystalline dry? Well
below in the struts of laundry is the four-wheel drive

vehicle in which to make an expedition
to the bush, or as we now say the Land,
the three quarters of our continent
set aside for mystic poetry.

The Edgeless

Floodwater from remote rains has spread out
of the riverine scrub, resuming its mirages.
Mostly shallow, mild water
it ties its hidden drowning strains
taut around odd trees, in that low forest
whose skinny shade turns the water taupe. Nests float
and the vaster flat shine is cobbled at wave-shadow points
with little brown melons, just starting to smell rank.

The local station manager, his eyes
still squinting from the greenest green on the place,
the computer screen, strolls out of his office
onto the verandah. Tiny native bees
who fly standing up, like angels, shimmer the garden.
His wife points out their dog Boxer,
pads slipping, tongue slipping out, nails
catching in unseen lurch mineshafts, gamely
teetering along the round top rail of the killing yard.

Where does talk come from? the two ask each other
over teacups. — From the same place as the world.
We have got the word and we don't understand it.
It is like too much. — So we made up a word of our own
as much like nothing else as possible
and gave it to the machines. It made them grow —
And now we can't see the limits of that word either.

Come down off there, Boxer! Who put you up there?

The Drugs of War

On vinegar and sour fish sauce Rome's legions stemmed avalanches
of whirling golden warriors whose lands furnished veterans' ranches;
when the warriors broke through at last, they'd invented sour mash
but they took to sugared wines and failed to hold the lands of hash.

By beat of drum in the wars of rum flogged peasant boys faced front
and their warrior chiefs conversed coolly, attired for the hunt
and tobacco came in, in a pipe of peace, but joined the pipes of war
as an after-smoke of battle, or over the maps before.

All alcohols, all spirits lost strength in the trenches, that belt-fed country
then morphine summoned warrior dreams in ruined and would-be gentry;
stewed tea and vodka and benzedrine helped quell that mechanized fury —
the side that won by half a head then provided judge and jury.

In the acid war the word was Score; rising helicopters cried Smack-Smack!
Boys laid a napalm trip on earth and tried to take it back
but the pot boiled over in the rear; fighters tripped on their lines of force
and victory went to the supple hard side, eaters of fish sauce.

The perennial war drugs are made in ourselves: sex and adrenalin,
blood, and the endomorphias that transmute defeat and pain
and others hardly less chemical: eagles, justice, loyalty, edge,
the Judas face of every idea, and the fish that ferments in the brain.

Letters to the Winner

After the war, and just after marriage and fatherhood
ended in divorce, our neighbour won the special lottery,
an amount then equal to fifteen years of a manager's
salary at the bank, or fifty years' earnings by
a marginal farmer fermenting his clothes in the black
marinade of sweat, up in his mill-logging paddocks.

The district, used to one mailbag, now received two
every mailday. The fat one was for our neighbour.
After a dip or two, he let these bags accumulate
around the plank walls of the kitchen, over the chairs
till on a rainy day, he fed the tail-switching calves,
let the bullocks out of the yard, and pausing at the door
to wash his hands, came inside to read the letters.

Shaken out in a vast mound on the kitchen table
they slid down, slithered to his fingers. *I have 7 children*
I am under the doctor if you could see your way clear
equal Pardners in the Venture God would bless you lovey
assured of our best service for a mere fifteen pounds down
remember you're only lucky I knew you from the paper straightaway

Baksheesh, hissed the pages as he flattened them, baksheesh!
mate if your interested in a fellow diggers problems
old mate a friend in need — the Great Golden Letter
having come, now he was being punished for it.
You sound like a lovely big boy we could have such times
her's my photoe Doll Im wearing my birthday swimsuit
with the right man I would share this infallible system.

When he lifted the stove's iron disc and started feeding in
the pages he'd read, they clutched and streamed up the corrugated
black chimney shaft. And yet he went on reading,
holding each page by its points, feeling an obligation
to read each crude rehearsed lie, each come-on, flat truth, extremity:
We might visit you the wise investor a loan a bush man like you

remember we met on Roma Street for your delight and mine
a lick of the sultana — the white moraine kept slipping
its messages to him *you will be accursed* he husked them like cobs
Mr Nouveau Jack old man my legs are all paralysed up.
Black smuts swirled weightless in the room *some good kind person*
like the nausea of a novice free-falling in a deep mine's cage
now I have lost his pension and formed a sticky nimbus round him

but he read on, fascinated by a further human range
not even war had taught him, nor literature glossed for him
since he never read literature. Merely the great reject pile
which high style is there to snub and filter, for readers.
That his one day's reading had a strong taste of what he and war
had made of his marriage is likely; he was not without sympathy,

but his leap had hit a wire through which the human is policed.
His head throbbed as if busting with a soundless shout
of immemorial sobbed invective *God-forsaken, God-forsakin*
as he stopped reading, and sat blackened in his riches.

The China Pear Trees

The power of three China pear trees
standing in their splintery timber bark
on an open paddock:

the selector's house that staked and watered them
in Bible times, beside a spaded patch
proved deciduous; it went away in loads,

but after sixty years of standing out,
vanishing in autumn, blizzarding in spring,
among the farmlands' sparse and giant furniture,

after sixty crops gorged on from all directions,
so that no windfalls, fermenting, shrank to lizard-skinned
puree in the short grazed grass,

the trees drew another house, electrified and steaming
but tin-roofed as before for blazing clouds to creak over
and with tiny nude frogs upright again on lamplit glass;

they drew another kitchen garden, and a dam
half scintillating waterlily pleasance, half irrigation,
an ad hoc orchard, Christmas pines, a cud-dropping mower;

they drew a wire fence around acres of enclosure
shaped like a fuel tin, its spout a tunnel of trees
tangled in passionflower and beige-belled wonga vine,

down inside which a floodtime waterfall churns
millet-sized gravel. And they called lush water-leaved trees
like themselves to the stumpholes of gone rainforest

to shade with four seasons the tattered evergreen
oil-haloed face of a subtle fire landscape
(water forest versus fire forest, ancient war of the southern world).

It was this shade in the end, not their coarse bottling fruit
that mirrored the moist creek trees outward, as a culture
containing the old gardener now untying and heaping up

one more summer's stems and chutneys,
his granddaughter walking a horse the colour of her boots
and his tree-shaping son ripping out the odd failed seedling,
"Sorry, tree. I kill and I learn."

The Vol Sprung from Heraldry

Left wing, right wing:
two wings torment our lives,
two wings without a body,
joined, turkey wing and vulture wing

like the badge of an airborne army.
Each has its clients to enfold
and shed lice on. It gets quite underarm
and the other wing lashes at them.

Two wings without a bird —
it is called a *vol* in heraldry —
spinning, fighting, low to the ground,
whomping up evil dusts for our breath.

Sometimes they borrow a head
like the bride-head on a Scots grave,
stone, pitiless in pursed absorption,
drinking blood to digest into thought,

biting out sinews to weave
into an agenda of trap questions.
Only on abstract figures,
statues of the past or future

does it have mercy.
Discarded, it drops from the wings
to burst in the street like a car bomb
— and the lightened, whipping

wings stiffen to a double kinked sword,
left tip up, right point down
in wingovers shedding diseased feathers
and the slashed air bleeds oppression.

Two wings, longing for a body:
left wing, right wing, flexing
still from the noble secret spring
that launched, propels and will exhaust them:

that everything in the end grows boring.

The Megaethon: 1850, 1906-29

i.m. Leo Port

Farmer Cleve, gent., of the Hunter
Valley has ordained that his large
Sydney-built steam engine shall be walked
home under its own power, on iron
shoes serially laid beneath its wheels.
Making four miles a day, it's no fizzer.
He has christened it the Megaethon,
Greek for the Ruddy Big Fiery Thing.

On black iron plates that lean down
and flatten successively, imprinting
rectangular billets of progression
it advances on the Hawkesbury district
hissing, clanking, stoked by freed men.
People run from oat-field and wash-house,
from pot-house and cockpit to gape
at its shackled gait, its belt-drive pulsation:

"Look, Mother, it walks on its knees!" "Aye,
it's praying its way to Wiseman's Ferry,
coughing black smoke out of its steeple!"
Sparks canter by it, cracking whips. Small
native children scream "Buggy-buggy!"
and the iron gangs straighten from their sad
triangular thoughts to watch another
mighty value approach along their spadework.

In that last, dissolving convict year
what passes their wedged grins is a harbinger
not merely of words like *humdinger*, but
of stumpjump ploughs, metal ores made float,
ice plants, keel wings, a widening vote,
the world's harvesters, the utility truck, rotary
engines pipemoulds lawnmowers — this motor the
slaves watch strikes a ringing New World note.

As, tilting, stayed with ropes and pulleys,
the Megaethon descends a plateau edge,
casting shoes, crushing sandstone, only
the poorest, though, watching from dry bush
in that chain-tugging year, last before the gold rush,
know that here is a centre of the world
and that one who can rattle the inverted
cosmos is stamping to her stamping ground.

Not guided by such truth, the Megaethon
veers towards rum-and-opium stops,
waits, cooling, beside a slab bordello
and leans at last in upland swamp,
flat-footed, becoming salvage,
freight for ribald bullockies. Its polygonal
rhythms will engender no balladry;
it won't break the trench-lines at Vicksburg.

The engine goes home to make chaff
and the idea of the Megaethon
must travel underground. Stockmen gallop
above it. It travels underground.
Secret ballots and boxkites are invented,
unions form, national purposes gather
above it. It travels underground;
for fifty years it travels underground

losing its first name. It surfaces
in Melbourne at last, in the mind
of one Frank Bettrill, who calls
his wheel of three sliding plates
the Pedrail or Dreadnaught wheel
"for travelling across country in all
conditions, where roads may be absent."
In all but name, the Megaethon

is abroad again, now clearing country,
now ploughing the new farms. Its jointed
wheel-plates go to war on artillery
lashing back the Ottoman Empire
from Suez to Damascus. The monster
guns of Flanders advance and recoil
on many-slatted wheels. Tanks grind by them,
collateral descendants of the Megaethon

which itself remains in innocent
rebirth in its own hemisphere.
Its largest example, Big Lizzie
spends the mid-war years crossing Victoria
and following the Murray through Gunbower,
Mystic Park and Day Trap to Mildura.
From its cab eighteen feet above ground
crews wave to the river paddlesteamers:

"Gutter sailors! Our ship don't *need* water!"
Submarine in the mallee forests
Big Lizzie leaves a shattered wake;
she wades marsh, crosses grass fires' negative
landscape: black ground, bleached rattling trees;

her slamming gait shuts the earth down
but her following ploughs reopen it
in long rising loaves. Soldiers follow her

and turn into farmers sewing full
wheat bags with a large darning needle.
Giant workhorse born between the ages
of plodding feet and highway speeds
it takes lorries a decade to catch
and relegate Lizzie's oil-engined shuffle.
The Megaethon thus re-enters quaintness
at two miles an hour, having,

though ponderous, only lightly existed
(twice so far) and never directly
shed. blood. And there, repaired with wire
from strict fences, it still walks the trackless,
slow as workaday, available for metaphor,
laying down and picking up the squeezed-
fragrant iron suit-cards of its patience,
crews making mugs of tea from its boiler.

Fastness

I am listening for words the eldest
of three brothers must have uttered
magically, out of their whole being

to make a sergeant major look down
at the stamped grass, and not have them stopped
as they walked, not trooped, off his shouting
showground parade, in the brown
fatal clothes and pink boots they'd been given,

to retrieve their own horses and vanish
bearing even the unloaded strap rifles
the Government would still be pursuing
a decade later, along with the brothers.

I have come as far as officials
and sergeants ever came, telling their
hillbilly yarns: the boy-headed calf,
the barbed wire across the teenage bedroom,
the dead wife backpacked forty miles
in a chaff bag, but gutted to save weight.
I have passed where their cars' spoke-wheels
slid and stopped, and the silent vines hung.

Since beyond the exact words, I need
the gesture with which they were said,
the horizons and hill air that shaped them,
the adze-faceted timbers of the kitchen
where they were repeated to the old people

who, having heard nothing about war,
had sent the boys three days round trip
in to town for saltpetre and tobacco.
I need the angle of cloud forest
visible through that door, the fire chains
and the leaf tastes of tank water there.

I will only have history, lacking these,
not the words as they have to be
spoken out, in such moments:

centrally, so as to pass the mind
of cheerful blustering authority
and paralyse it in its dream —

right in the unmeant nick of time
even as the rails were shutting
on the wide whooping yard of adventure
and making it a cattle chute
that led through jokes and accoutrements
to the long blood trail a-winding.

I need not think the brothers were
unattracted by a world venture
in aid of the woman Belgium
or not drawn by herd-warmth towards
the glorious manhunting promised them
by fellows round pipe-drawing fires
outside the beast-pavilions they slept in.

I need remember only the angel
poverty wrestles with in vast places
to know the power of abandon
people want, with control, to touch
when they tell hillbilly stories

and knowing it well, to uncover
how the brothers missed their legendary
Anzac chance, I need only
sit on this rusty bedstead, on a known
vanished sleepout verandah and reflect

how the lifelong lordly of space
might speak, in discernment of spirits
at the loud surcingled overseer's
very first bawled genial insult
to any of theirs. Not the camel's-back-
breaking, trapped slight, but the first.

1980 in a Street of Federation Houses

In 1980, in a street of Federation houses
a man is brushing his hair inside a car
while waiting for his children. It is his access day.

Men down the street — one perched high
as an oldtime sailor, others hauling long lines —
are dismantling a tree, from the top down. A heavy
branch drops, out of keen gristing noise, and runs
dragging all the stumpy hauliers
inwards on their ropes, then hangs swinging.

In 1964, the same man, slightly plumper
is proclaiming in the Union bar *Now let*
us watch the angels dance on the head of a pill!
He does not mean, but swallows, a methedrine tablet.

In the same year he consents for the first time
to find the woodchoppers at the Easter Show
faintly comical, in their cricketing whites and singlets,

starting in handicap order to knock on wood:
one chopper, two choppier, then a clobbering
increment of cobbers, down in the grunting arena —

he assigns them to 1955, an obsolete year
and the whole Labor Movement
shifts and re-levels in his mind
like mercury, needing new calibrations.

In 1824 in another country
present to his albums, small children run all day
breathing lint in a cavernous tropic factory
lit by weak globes on which older lint has caramelled.

They work from dawn to palm-frond-clattering dark
loading bales of packaged shirts on to trucks
driven by tribesmen who smoke, as they do themselves,
like the Industrial Revolution, paper chimneys in their cursing mouths.

Upcountry, men of the Thirties in 1950s uniform
instruct youths and girls of the starving fourteen hundreds
how to conjure with rifles the year Seventeen Ninety-two.
Their ammunition is the first packaged goods they have handled.

To reproduce yourself is to admit defeat!
His dashing friend had said it, in the year

he was told about cadmium fish, and blamed for the future.
To reproduce oneself? Who ever did that?

Most perhaps, before the Industrial Revolution
but then permanent death came in; all the years,
all the centuries now had to fit into one lifetime.

As did heaven. Which drew hell.
The Bomb and the Club Méditerranée had to lie
down together —. He begins to see his educators
as missionaries of the new unending death.

He shifts to another year, along the band
of his car's stereo, and his children are playing
in a tent on sandy grass;
can there be a time in which this scene is not a bibelot?

Now that up the suburban street that leads to the past
a figure is leading not greyhounds but Afghan hounds
and on the beach beyond, women who enter the surf
shielding a web of dusty lint emerge
and each is wearing a feather!

The Milk Lorry

Now the milk lorry is a polished submarine
that rolls up at midday, attaches a trunk and inhales
the dairy's tank to a frosty snore in minutes

but its forerunner was the high-tyred barn of crisp mornings,
reeking Diesel and mammary, hazy in its roped interior
as a carpet under beaters, as it crashed along potholed lanes

cooeeing at schoolgirls. Long planks like unshipped oars
butted, levelling in there, because between each farm's
stranded wharf of milk cans, the work was feverish slotting

of floors above floors, for load. It was sling out the bashed
paint-collared empties and waltz in the full,
stumbling on their rims under ribaldry, tilting their big gallons

then the schoolboy's calisthenic, hoisting steel men man-high
till the glancing hold was a magazine of casque armour,
a tinplate tween-decks, a seminar engrossed

in one swaying tradition, behind the speeding doorways
that tempted a truant to brace and drop, short of town
and spend the day, with book or not, down under

the bridge of a river that by dinnertime would be
tongueing like cattledogs, or down a moth-dusty reach
where the fish-feeding milk boat and cedar barge once floated.

The Butter Factory

It was built of things that must not mix:
paint, cream and water, fire and dusty oil.
You heard the water dreaming in its large
kneed pipes, up from the weir. And the cordwood
our fathers cut for the furnace stood in walls
like the sleeper-stacks of a continental railway.

The cream arrived in lorried tides; its procession
crossed a platform of workers' stagecraft: *Come here
Friday-Legs! Or I'll feel your hernia* —
Overalled in milk's colour, men moved the heart of milk,
separated into thousands, along a roller track — *Trucks?
That one of mine, son, it pulls like a sixteen-year-old* —
to the tester who broached the can lids, causing fat tears,
who tasted, dipped and did his thin stoppered chemistry
on our labour, as the empties chattered downstage and fumed.

Under the high roof, black-crusted and stainless steels
were walled apart: black romped with leather belts
but paddlewheels sailed the silvery vats where muscles
of the one deep cream were exercised to a bullion
to be blocked in paper. And between waves of delivery
the men trod on water, hosing the rainbows of a shift.

It was damp April even at Christmas round every
margin of the factory. Also it opened the mouth
to see tackles on glibbed gravel, and the mossed char louvres
of the ice-plant's timber tower streaming with
heavy rain all day, above the droughty paddocks
of the totem cows round whom our lives were dancing.

Bats' Ultrasound

Sleeping-bagged in a duplex wing
with fleas, in rock-cleft or building
radar bats are darkness in miniature,
their whole face one tufty crinkled ear
with weak eyes, fine teeth bared to sing.

Few are vampires. None flit through the mirror.
Where they flutter at evening's a queer
tonal hunting zone above highest C.
Insect prey at the peak of our hearing
drone re to their detailing tee:

ah, eyrie-ire; aero hour, eh?
O'er our ur-area (our era aye
ere your raw row) we air our array,
err, yaw, row wry — aura our orrery,
our eerie ü our ray, our arrow.

A rare ear, our aery Yahweh.

Roman Cage-cups

Excavate, at a constant curving interval
a layer of air between the inner and outer
skins of a glass beaker, leaving only odd struts integral;

at the same time, at the same ablative atom-
by-atom rate, sculpt the outer shell to an openwork
of rings, or foliage, or a muscular Elysium —

It made for calm paste and a steady file
that one false stroke, one twitch could cost a year's time,
a good billet, your concubine. Only the cups were held noble.

Plebs and immigrants fashioned them, punters
who ate tavern-fried pike and talked Vulgate.
The very first might have been made as a stunt, as

the life-gambit of a slave. Or a joke on the feasting scene:
a wine-bowl no one coarsely drunk could handle
nor, since baseless, easily put down,

a marvel of undercutting, a glass vessel
so costly it would exact that Roman gravity,
draw blood, and feud, if grasped without suavity.

The one depicting Thracian Lycurgus
strangled by amorous vines for slighting Bacchus
could hardly have survived an old-time bacchanal.

Where polish is cutting and festivity an ice
and most meaning paradox, it is an age of cool.
Culture has lifted off and impends above us

on brittle legs, always more or less transparent.
Splendour of social vertigo. Even to describe it serves its luxury.
But this is the fourth, that is, the eleventh century:

war-chiefs are coming whose descendants in turn
will learn to exalt, to suspend the new fraternal
faith that triumphed lately. So the engravers groove on

under the fixed heavens, into that driest liquid,
miming a low but vast space, never roofed entirely —
as between the idea and its word, a global interstice.

The glass flowers of Harvard, monks' micro pen-lace, a chromosome
needled to grow wings on a horse (which they'd also have done),
the freely moving ivory dragons-inside-a-dragon

ball of Cathay — the impossible is a groove:
why else do we do it? Even some given a choice
would rather work the metaphors than live them, in society.

But nothing, since sparkle became permanent in the thumbs
and rib-cages of these craftsmen, has matched their handiwork
for gentleness, or edge. They put the gape into agapé,

these factory products, of all Rome's underground Gothic:
cups transfigured by hand, too delicate to break.
Some, exported beyond the Rhine as a *miss-*

ion civilisatrice, have survived complete and unchipped
a sesquimillennium longer than the trumpets (allude,
allude) of the arena. Rome's very hardest rock.

The Lake Surnames

There are rental houseboats down the lakes now.
Two people facing, with drinks, in a restaurant party
talk about them: *That idiot, he ran us aground*
in the dark! These fishermen rescued us,
towed us off the mudbank. They were frightening actually,
real inbred faces, Deliverance people
when we saw them by torchlight in their boat —

    For an instant, rain rattles at the glass
    and brown cardboards of a kitchen window
    and drips lamplight-coloured out of soot
    in the fireplace, hitching steam off stove-iron.

    Tins of beeswax, nails and poultice mixture
    stick to shelves behind the door. Triangular
    too, the caramel dark up under rafters
    is shared, above one plank wall, by the room

    where the English housekeeper screamed
    at a crisp bat on the lino. Guest room,
    parents' room, always called *the room*
    with tennis racquet and rifle in the lowboy.

    Quick steps jingle the glassed cabinet
    as a figure fishes spoons from scalding water
    ("what's not clean's sterilised") in the board-railed
    double triangle of a kerosene-tin sink,

    a real Bogan sink, on the table.
    The upright wireless, having died when valves vanished
    has its back to the wall. It is a *plant* for money
    guarded by a nesting snake, who'll be killed when discovered.

    The new car outside, streaming cricket scores
    is a sit-in radio, glowing, tightly furnished
    but in the Auburn wood stove, the fire laps
    and is luxury too, in one of them flood years

— With only the briefest pause, the other
answers: *There aren't that many full-time*
surnames down the lakes. If you'd addressed them
as Mr Blanche, Mr Woodward, Mr Legge,
Mr Bramble, or Palmer, your own surname
you'd probably have been right. And more at ease.

Nocturne

Brisbane, night-gathered, far away
estuarine imaginary city
of houses towering down one side
of slatted lights seen under leaves

confluence of ranginess with lush,
Brisbane, of rotogravure memory
approached by web lines of coke and grit
by sleepers racked in corridor trains

weatherboard incantatory city
of the timber duchess, the strapped port
in Auchenflower and Fortitude Valley
and bottletops spat in Vulture Street

greatest of the floodtime towns
that choked the dictionary with silt
and hung a navy in the tropic gardens.
Brisbane, on the steep green slope to war

brothel-humid headquarters city
where commandos and their allies fought
down café stairs, belt buckle and boot
and once with a rattletrap green gun.

In midnight nets, in mango bombings
Brisbane, storied and cable-fixed
above your rum river, farewell and adieu
in marble on the hill of Toowong

by golfing pockets, by deep squared pockets
night heals the bubbled tar of day
and the crab moon, rising, reddens above
Brisbane, rotating far away.

Lotus Dam

Lotus leaves, standing feet above the water
collect at their centre a perfect lens of rain
and heel, and tip it back into the water.

Their baby leaves are feet again, or slant lips
scrolled in declaration; pointed at toe and heel
they echo an unwalked sole in their pale green crinkles

and under blown and picket blooms, the floor
of floating leaves rolls light rainwater marbles
back and forth on sharkskins of anchored rippling.

Each speculum, pearl and pebble of the first water
rides, sprung with weight, on its live mirroring skin
tipped green and loganberry, till one or other sky

redeems it, beneath bent foils and ferruled canes
where cupped pink bursts all day, above riddled water.

At Min-Min Camp

In the afternoon, a blue storm walloped and split
like a loose mainsail behind us. Then another
far out on the plain fumed its corrugated walls.

A heavy dough of cloud kept rising, and reached us.
The speeding turbid sky went out of focus, fracturing
continually, and poured. We made camp on a verandah

that had lost its house. I remembered it: pitsawn pine
lined with newspaper. People lived on treacle and rabbit
by firelight, and slept under grain-bag quilts there.

It was a lingering house. Millions had lived there
on their way to the modern world. Now they longed for and feared it.
It had been the last house, and the first.

Dark lightnings tore the ground as we ripped up firewood
and when the rain died away to conversation, and parted
on refreshed increasing star-charts, there arose

an unlikely bushfire in the ranges. The moon leaped from it,
slim, trim in perfect roundness. Spiderwebs palely yellow
by firelight changed sides, and were steel thread, diamante.

Orange gold itself, everything the moon gave, everywhere
was nickel silver, or that lake-submerged no-colour
native to dreams. Sparse human lights on earth

were solar-coloured, though: ingots of a homestead,
amoebae that moved and twinned on distant roads
and an unfixed anomaly, like a star with land behind it.

We were drinking tea round a sheet-iron fire on the boards
bearing chill on our shoulders, like the boys who'd slept
on that verandah, and gone to be wandering lights

lifelong on the plains. You can't catch up to them now
though it isn't long ago: when we came from the Rift Valley
we all lived in a small star on the ground.

From the Rift we also carried the two kinds of fear
humans inherit: the rational kind, facing say weapons
and the soul's kind, the creeps. Awe, which warns of law.

The two were long bound together, in the sacred
cultures of fright, that called shifting faces to the light's edge:
none worse than our own, when we came dreaming of houses.

Then the sacred turned fairytale, as always. And the new thing,
holiness, a true face, constant in all lights,
was still very scattered. It saved some. It is still scattered.

Many long for the sacred lights, and would renew their lore
in honoured bantustans — no faery for the laager of the lagerphone —
but they are unfixed now, and recede, and suddenly turn pale as

an escaped wife dying of a dread poem. Or her child
who sniffs his petrol, and reels like a shot kangaroo:
something else, and not the worst, that happens in a shifting light.

Holiness is harder to inhale, for adventure or desperation.
It cleanses awe of fear, though not of detailed love,
the nomads' other linkage, and maps the law afresh with it.

We left that verandah next day, and its ruined garden
of wire and daylilies, its grassy fringe of ancient pee scalds
and travelled further west on a truck that had lost its body.

Hearing Impairment

Hearing loss? Yes, loss is what we hear
who are starting to go deaf. Loss
trails a lot of weird puns in its wake, viz.
Dad's a real prism of the Left —
you'd like me to repeat that?
THE SAD SURREALISM OF THE DEAF.

It's mind over mutter at work
guessing half what the munglers are saying
and society's worse. Punchlines elude to you
as Henry Lawson and other touchy drinkers
have claimed. Asides, too, go pasture.
It's particularly nasty with a wether.

First you crane at people, face them
while you can still face them. But grudgually
you give up dinnier parties; you begin
to think about Beethoven; you Hanover
next visit here on silly Narda Fearing — I SAY
YOU CAN HAVE AN EXQUISITE EAR
AND STILL BE HARD OF HEARING.

It seems to be mainly speech, at first,
that escapes you — and that can be a rest,
the poor man's escape itch from Babel.
You can still hear a duck way upriver,
a lorry miles off on the highway. You
can still say boo to a goose and
read its curt yellow-lipped reply.
You can shout SING UP to a magpie,

but one day soon you must feel
the silent stopwatch chill your ear
in the doctor's rooms, and be wired
back into a slightly thinned world
with a faint plastic undertone to it
and, if the rumours are true, snatches
of static, music, police transmissions:
it's a BARF minor Car Fourteen prospect.

But maybe hearing aids are now perfect
and maybe it's not all that soon.
Sweet nothings in your ear are still sweet;
you've heard the human range by your age
and can follow most talk from memory;
the peace of the graveyard's well up
on that of the grave. And the world would
enjoy peace and birdsong for more moments

if you were head of government, enquiring
of an aide Why, Simpkins, do you tell me
a warrior is a ready flirt?
I might argue — and flowers keep blooming
as he swallows his larynx to shriek
our common mind-overloading sentence:
I'M SORRY, SIR, IT'S A RED ALERT!

At Thunderbolt's Grave in Uralla

The New England Highway was formed
by Christian men who reckoned
Adam and Eve should have been
sodomized for the curse of work
they brought on humankind,
not drudgery, but work.
No luxury of distinctions.

None ever went to Bali. Some set out.
But roads were game reserves to Thunderbolt
when a bridge was a leap, and wheels
were laborious, trundling through the splashways.
There were two heights of people: equestrians
and those foreshortened on foot.
All were more dressed, because more naked.

That German brass band that Thunderbolt,
attended by a pregnant boy,
bailed up on Goonoo Goonoo Gap:
"Gentlemen, if you are that poor
I'll refund your twenty pound, provided
a horse I mean to shake wins at Tenterfield."
And it did, arching its neck, and he did
by postal note at Warwick.
Hoch! Public relations by trombone!

No convict ever got off Cockatoo
Island by swimming except Thunderbolt.
His lady, Yellow Long or Long Yella,
whichever way the name points, swam
the channel from Balmain before him
bringing tucker and clothes, and she got
him past the sharks when he swam for it.

But who wouldn't swim, and wear trousers
for a man pinched and bearded as the nine
lions on the courthouse coat of arms
with their tongues saying languish and lavish,
who took her from men who gasped romance
into her lungs and offered sixpence,
from her own heart-gelded tribesfolk
and white women's dreadful eyes?

Though Uralla creek is floored with planks now
the amethystine light of New England
still seems augmented from beneath
both horizons; tin outside chimneys

still squeeze woodsmoke into the air
but the police cars come wailing their
unerotic In-Out In-Out,
red-shifting over Goonoo Goonoo.

Of all the known bushrangers,
those cropped in the floggers' gulag,
those jostled by its Crown guards,
the bolters and the hoods were merely shot
or ironed or hanged. Only three required
frenzied extermination, with rituals:
Jackey Westaway, made monstrous by torture,
Fred Ward shot and head-pulped, Ben Hall
shot dead, and for several minutes afterwards.

All three were thieves. They likely never met.
All three stole the Crown's magic pallium
and trailed it through the bush, a drag
for raging pursuit. On every snag
they left some white or blue — the red part
they threw away at once, disdaining murder.
Robbery with mock menaces? Why that is subsidy!
The part they died hard for was the part
they wouldn't play, not believing the game worth murder.

Criminal noncomplicity! It was something nameless
above all stations, that critical magic
haloed in laughter. *Tell Fred I need to be robbed Friday
or I'm jiggered!* A deadly style suddenly felt lumbering,
battered with a slapstick. Our only indigenous revolution.
It took Ned Kelly to reassure policemen.

Why don't we kill like Americans?
We started to. The police were pushing it
but we weren't a republic for bringing things to a head
and these, even dying — *Are you a married man?*
cried Ward, and fired wide — helped wrong-foot mortal drama
and leave it decrepit, a police atmosphere.
In a few years, the game was boss and union.
Now society doesn't value individuals
enough for human sacrifice.

You were a cross swell, Fred. You alone never
used a gang. Those always kill, as Hall learned.
I hope your children found your cache
and did good with it. They left some on deposit.

Leaf Spring

The long-limbed hills recline high
in Disposals khaki boiled in tankwater
or barbed-wire-tattered navy wool.
A dust of oil blues the farther air.

Crotches of black shade timber
thicken, and walled sky insets;
friezes of the one tree are repeated
along ridgelines, and the gesture of the heights

continues beneath the valley floor,
outcrops stepping toward the roofed creeks'
greener underground forest, spacing
corrugated corn flats. Contour-line by contour

cattle walk the hills, in a casual-seeming
prison strung from buried violins.
Sparse houses sit unpacked for good, each
among sheds, in its wheeltracked star.

Hobnail and elastic-side, bare and cloven feet:
you can't know this landscape in shoes, or with ideas
like relevance. It is a haughty pastoral
bent fitfully to farming's fourteen-hour days.

Disked-up ground in unseasonable heat
burns purple, and the tracks of a foam-white
longed-for watersnake are brown down every incline.
Season of smoke and parrots pecking the road,

half-naturalised autumn. Fruit is almost done
though few deciduous imports have yet decided;
no rain, and the slow tanks fill with dew;
nothing flowering, yet colour is abundant:

it is leaf spring, that comes on after heat.
The paperbark trees that suck on swampy clay
are magnified in skims of leek and sherry.
Though growth's gone out of grass, and cattle nose

green from underneath its tawny pelt,
the creek trees cluster, showered with pale expansion
from inside themselves, as if from dreams of rain;
heightening gumtrees are tipped bronze and citrine

and grey-barked apple trees are misted round
with rosy blue — the aged angophora trees
that sprout from every live part of themselves
and drop their heavy death along the ground

on just such a still day here
as shade broadens south of everything
and fugitive whisky-bottle blink
and windscreen glance point the paddock air.

Infra Red

for Prof. Fred Hoyle and the IRAS telescope

Dark stars that never fire,
brown dwarfs, whose deepening collapse
inward on themselves never tightens to fuse glory,
scorched dust the size of worlds, and tenuous
sandbars strung between the galaxies,
a universe dull with life:

with the eye and eye-adjuncts
mind sees only what is burning, the peak nodes of fury
that make all spiralling in on them
or coronally near, blowing outward from them,
look eager, intense, even brave. Most of the real
however is obscurely reflective, just sauntering along,
yarning across a ditch, or watching television,
vaguely dreaming, perhaps about pubic stuff,

getting tea ready. This absorbs most of the light
but is also family. It impoverishes to unreality
not to consider the dim, cannon fodder of stardom,
the gravities they are steepening to,
the unfathomable from which the trite is spoken.
And starry science is an evening paper astrology
without the unknown bodies registered
only by total pain, only by dazzled joy,
the transits marked by a tight grip of the heart.

That the visible stars are suburbs and slow towns
hyped to light speed is the testimony of debris
and the serious swarms at rest in migrant trajectories.
Brilliance stands accused of all their losses.
Presence perhaps, and the inference of presence,
not light, should found a more complete astronomy.

It will draw in absence, too:
the pain-years between a love and its fulfilment,
the intricate spiral space of suppressed tradition
and all the warmth, whose peaks aren't those of heat,
that the white dwarfs froze out of their galaxies.

Poetry and Religion

Religions are poems. They concert
our daylight and dreaming mind, our
emotions, instinct, breath and native gesture

into the only whole thinking: poetry.
Nothing's said till it's dreamed out in words
and nothing's true that figures in words only.

A poem, compared with an arrayed religion,
may be like a soldier's one short marriage night
to die and live by. But that is a small religion.

Full religion is the large poem in loving repetition;
like any poem, it must be inexhaustible and complete
with turns where we ask Now why did the poet do that?

You can't pray a lie, said Huckleberry Finn;
you can't poe one either. It is the same mirror:
mobile, glancing, we call it poetry,

fixed centrally, we call it a religion,
and God is the poetry caught in any religion,
caught, not imprisoned. Caught as in a mirror

that he attracted, being in the world as poetry
is in the poem, a law against its closure.
There'll always be religion around while there is poetry

or a lack of it. Both are given, and intermittent,
as the action of those birds — crested pigeon, rosella parrot —
who fly with wings shut, then beating, and again shut.

When Bounty is Down to Persimmons and Lemons

In May, Mary's month
when snakes go to sleep,
sunlight and shade lengthen,
forest grows deep,

wood coughs at the axe
and splinters hurt worse,
barbed wire pulls through
every post in reverse,

old horses grow shaggy
and flies hunker down
on curtains, like sequins
on a dead girl's ball gown.

Grey soldier-birds arrive
in flickers of speed
to hang upside down
from a quivering weed

or tremble trees' foliage
that they trickle down through.
Women's Weekly summer fashions
in the compost turn blue.

The sun slants in under things
and stares right through houses;
soon pyjamas will peep, though,
from the bottoms of trousers.

Night-barking dogs quieten
as overcast forms
and it rains, with far thunder
in queer predawn storms;

then the school bus tops ridges
with clay marks for effort,
picking up drowsy schoolkids,
none of them now barefoot,

and farmers take spanners
to the balers, gang ploughs
and towering diesel tractors
they prefer to their cows.

The Kitchens

This deep in the year, in the frosts of then,
that steeled sheets left ghostly on the stayed line,
smoked over verandah beds, cruelled water taps rigid,
family and visitors would sit beside the lake
of blinding coals, that end of the detached kitchen,
the older fellows quoting qoph *and* resh
from the Book of Psalms, as they sizzled phlegm
(some still did it after iron stoves came
and the young moved off to cards and the radio)
and all told stories. That's a kind of spoken video:

> We rode through from the Myall
> on that road of the cedarcutter's ghost.
> All this was called Wild Horses Creek then;
> you could plait the grass over the pommel
> of your saddle. That grass don't grow now.
> I remember we camped on Waterloo that night
> there where the black men gave the troopers a hiding.

If you missed anything: plough,
saddle, cornplanter, shovel,
you just went across to Uncle Bob's
and brought it home. If he
was there, he never looked ashamed:
he'd just tell you a joke,
some lies, sing you a poem,
keep you there drinking all night —

> The garden was all she had; the parrots were at it
> and she came out and said to them, quite serious
> like as if to reasonable people They are *my* peas.
> And do you know? They flew off and never come back.

Bloody cruel mongrels, telling me the native bear
would grow a new pelt if you skun it alive.
Everybody knows that, they told me. I told them
if I caught any man skinning bears alive
on my place, he'd bloody need a new hide himself.

> Tommy Turpin the blackfellow said to me More better
> you walk behind me today, boss.
> Might be devil-devil tell me hit you with the axe
> longa back of the head. I thought he was joking
> then I saw he wasn't. My word I stayed behind
> that day, with the axe, trimming tongues on the rails
> while he cut mortises out of the posts. I listened.

I wis eight year old, an Faither gied me the lang gun
tae gang doon an shuit the native hens at wis aitin
aa oor oats. I reasoned gin ye pit ae chairge
i the gun, pouder waddin an shot, ye got ae shot
sae pit in twa, ye'd get twa. Aweel, I pit in seven,
liggd doon ahint a stump, pu'd the trigger — an the warld
gaed milky white. I think I visited Scotland
whaur I had never been. It wis a ferlie I wis seean.
It wis a sonsy place. But Granny gard me gang back.
Mither wis skailan watter on ma heid, greetin. Aa they found
o the gun wis stump-flinders, but there wis a black scour through the oats,
an unco ringan in ma ears, an fifteen deid native hens.

    Of course long tongue she laughed about that other
    and they pumped her about you can guess and hanging round there
    and she said He's got one on him like a horse, Mama,
    and I like it. Well! And all because of you know —

Father couldn't stand meanness.
When Uncle you-know-who
charged money for milking our cows
that time Isabel was took bad
Father called him gutless,
not just tin-arsed, but gutless.
Meanness is for cowards, Father reckoned.

    The little devil, he says to the minister's wife
    Daddy reckons we can't have any more children,
    we need the milk for the pigs. Dear I was mortified —

Poor Auntie Mary was dying Old and frail
all scroopered down in the bedclothes pale as cotton
even her hardworking old hands Oh it was sad
people in the room her big daughters performing
rattling the bedknobs There is a white angel
in the room says Mary in this weird voice And then
NO! she heaves herself up Bloody no! Be quiet!
she coughed and spat Phoo! I'll be damned if I'll die!
She's back making bread the next week Lived ten more years.

    Well it was black Navy rum; it buggered Darcy.
    Fell off his horse, crawled under the cemetery fence.
    Then some yahoos cantered past Yez all asleep in there?
    All but me, croaks Darcy. They off at a hand gallop,
    squealing out, and his horse behind them, stirrups belting it.

The worst ghost I ever saw
was a policeman and (one of the squatters)
moving cattle at night.
I caught them in my headlights.

It haunted me. Every time
I went in to town after that
somehow I'd get arrested —

I'll swear snakes have got no brains!
That carpet snake we had in the rafters
to eat rats, one day it et a chook.
I killed it with the pitchfork, ran a tine
through the top of its head, and chucked it
down the gully. It was back in a week
with a scab on its head and another under its chin.
They bring a house good luck but they got no brain.

Then someone might cup his hand short of the tongue
of a taut violin, try each string to be wrung
by the bow, that spanned razor of holy white hair
and launch all but his earthly weight into an air
that breathed up hearth fires strung worldwide between
the rung hills of being and the pearled hills of been.
In the language beyond speaking they'd sum the grim law,
speed it to a daedaly and foot it to a draw,
the tones of their scale five gnarled fingers wide
and what sang were all angles between love and pride.

Inverse Ballad

Grandfather's grandfather rode down from New England
that terrible steep road. One time there, his horse
shat over his shoulder. It's not so steep now.
Anyway he was riding, and two fellows came
out of the brush with revolvers pointed at him:

Bail up! What joy have you got for the poor, eh?
Bail up? Ye're never bushrangers? Wad ye shoot me?
My oath we'd shoot yer —. He looked them up and down,
poor weedy toerags both. Ye'd really shoot, then?
Masel, I never find it necessary.

Eh? You're on our lay, are you? — Aye, I am.
Ward's the name. — Not Thunderbolt? By Hell. Hmm.
They muttered some asides. Well, Mister Ward, you
are money on the hoof. A thousand's a fair screw
for turning you in. Dead *or* alive, so ride!

We're going to town to sell your pretty hide.
It must have felt lonely, riding ahead of them
knowing they could just as easily turn you in,
head lolling and blood dripping, strapped over your saddle.
When they reached the police post, the old sergeant listened

a moment, then snapped: Ye'll gie me thae barkers;
hand them over! Constable, handcuff yon men!
Ye ignorant puir loons, did ye no ken
Thunderbolt's no Scots. He disnae talk like me.
Ye'll hae time tae regret bailing up Mister Murray!

Ward's wintertime employer, had the police or he known.

56

Relics of Sandy

Beside the odd gene
just three pictures remain
of Uncle Sandy Beattie,
big fair man:

He used to swim his horse
through the flooded rivers
with bags tied on the saddle
when he was the mailman;
he'd hang on to its tail:
he couldn't swim at all.

Once for a bet he
humped a ton of iron
sheets up from the jetty
to the pub at Tinonee
and found a man had ridden
up, clinging on the load:
Ye've bowed my legs, laddie.

A loudmouth in the pub
was needling Sandy
one night, talking fight,
all the men he'd stiffened,
how the big raw ones were easy.
Yes, McMahon, I hear ye.
He finished his beer.
It's hard to take, McMahon,

and I'll not take any more.
Barman, give me a room key.
And he took the bareknuckle man
upstairs to the room,
pushed him in, locked the door:
Now, man, it's what you wanted,
no audience, we're private.
Just you and me for it!

There was thunder up there.
All the bottles jinked about
in the bar, and the fighter
squealed like a poor rabbit.
The barman got a pound
when Sandy came downstairs:
Yon man shouldn't have to
pay twice, for accommodation.
Sandy Beattie. Big fair man.

Joker as Told

Not a latch or lock could hold
a little horse we had,
not a gate or paddock.

He liked to get in the house.
Walk in, and you were liable
to find him in the kitchen
dribbling over the table
with a heap behind him

or you'd catch a hoof
right where it hurt bad
when you went in your bedroom.

He grew up with us kids,
played with us till he got rough.
Round then, they cut him,

but you couldn't ride him:
he'd bite your bum getting on,
kick your foot from the stirrup

and he could kick the spurs off
your boots. Almost hopped on with you,
and if he couldn't buck you
he'd lie down plop! and roll
in his temper, and he'd squeal.

He was from the Joker breed,
we called him Joker;
no joke much when he bit you
or ate the Monday washing.

They reckon he wanted to be
human, coming in the house.
I don't think so. I think he
wanted something people had.
He didn't do it from love of us.

He couldn't grow up to be a
full horse, and he wouldn't be a slave one.
I think he was looking for his childhood,
his foalhood and ours, when we played.

He was looking for the Kingdom of God.

Midwinter Haircut

Now the world has stopped. Dead middle of the year.
Cloud all the colours of a worn-out dairy bucket
freeze-frames the whole sky. The only sun is down
intensely deep in the dam's bewhiskered mirror
and the white-faced heron hides in the drain with her spear.

Now the world has stopped, doors could be left open.
Only one fly came awake to the kitchen heater
this breakfast time, and supped on a rice-bubble sluggishly.
No more will come inside out of the frost-crimped grass now.
Crime, too, sits in faraway cars. Phone lines drop at the horizon.

Now the world has stopped, what do we feel like doing?
The district's former haircutter, from the time before barbers, has shaved
and wants a haircut. So do I. No longer the munching hand clippers
with locks in their gears, nor the scissors more pointed than a beak
but the buzzing electric clipper, straight from its cardboard giftbox.

We'll sit under that on the broad-bottomed stool that was
the seat for sixty years of the district's only sit-down job,
the postmistress-telephonist's seat, where our poor great aunt
who trundled and spoke in sour verdicts sat to hand-crank
the tingling exchange, plugged us into each other's lives

and tapped consolation from gossip's cells as they unlidded.
From her shrewd kind successor who never tapped in, and planes
along below the eaves of our heads, we'll hear a tapestry
of weddings funerals surgeries, and after our sittings
be given a jar of pickle. Hers won't be like the house

a mile down the creek, where cards are cut and shuffled
in the middle of the day, and mortarbombs of beer
detonate the digestion, and they tell world-stopping yarns
like: I went to Sydney races. There along the rails,
    all snap brims and cold eyes, flanked by senior police

    and other, stony men with their eyes in a single crease
    stood the entire Government of New South Wales
    watching Narby ply the whip, all for show, over this fast colt.
    It was young and naive. It was heading for the post in a bolt
    while the filly carrying his and all the inside money

    strained to come level. Too quick for the stewards to note him
    Narby slipped the colt a low lash to the scrotum.
    It checked, shocked, stumbled — and the filly flashed by.

As he came from weighing in, I caught Narby's eye
and he said *Get out of it, mug,* quite conversationally. —

Forty Acre Ethno

The Easter rains are late this year
at this other end of a dry hard winter.
Low clouds grow great rustling crops of fall
and all the gully-courses braid and bubble,
their root-braced jugs and coarse lips pour
and it's black slog for cows when, grass lake to puddle,
a galloping dog sparks on all four.
It'll be plashy England here for a while
or boggy Scotland, by the bent straw colour
and the breaks of sun mirror-backed with chill.

Coming home? It was right. And it was time.
I had been twenty-nine years away
after books and work and society
but society vanished into ideology
and by then I could bring the other two home.
We haven't been out at night since we came
back, except last month, in the United Kingdom.
The towns ranged like footlights up the highway
and coastline here rehearse a subtle play
that's only staged in private by each family.

Sight and life restored by an eye operation
my father sits nightly before the glass screen
of a wood-burning slow combustion stove. We see
the same show, with words, on television.
Dad speaks of memories, and calls his fire homely:
when did you last hear that word without scorn
for something unglossy, or some poor woman?
Here, where thin is *poor,* and fat is *condition,*
"homely" is praise and warmth, spoken gratefully.
Its opposite lurks outside in dark blowing rain.

Horses are exposed to it, wanly stamping out
unglazed birth ware for mosquitoes in the coming season
and already peach trees are a bare wet frame
for notional little girls in pink dots of gingham.
Cars coming home fishtail and harrow the last mile,
their undersea headlights kicking gumtrees around eerily;
woodducks wake high in those trees, and peer from the door
they'll shove their ducklings out of, to spin down in their down,
sprawl, and swim to water. Our children dog the foot-
steps of their grandfather, learning their ancient culture.

The Climb Down

It seems the man who's been camping on the summit
of the Lucky Country Leisurecrafts building has elected
not to come down, or at least not tamely between the policemen
who now step out of the roof access doors. He waves
at them with — it looks at this distance like forgiveness,
and vaults the guardrail.
          The watchers' indrawn breaths
are a shout into themselves. He, call him now the fugitive,
eases down across a window, which swarms with bubble faces
as he leaves it. He drops. The swallowed shout bounces out —
and he grips a cornice. And draws his whole weight in
to a knot of rest there.
          Amplified negotiations now commence
but stay one-sided, slamming up the resonant verticals
for an hour. "Come on Spiderman! Come on there, blowfly!"
jeer some press-studded youths. "Remember who you're crawling for!"
At the end of an hour, he waves loud hailers silent
and descends another storey, on the hundred-year-old
walling of cream roughcast.
          He pauses for long minutes on the sill
of an office window. Workers will say he peered in
with the mild distortion of a face pressed to the glass
of an aquarium. His nose was a flat white circle,
his mouth made a fog patch. But now he drops away,
his fingers stabbing the wall all down the fitted
course of an inset drainpipe. His heels flirt with the crowd,
feeding ridged arcane rubber stamps to all the lenses.
He feasts now through glass on a tensed but unracking gym
as fire ladders develop upward.
          Crabbing sidelong, he evades them. A cherrypicker crane
extends its cup, but he waves that too to pass him by, as
he inches down into the zone of handlers and helpers.
"Enjoy it, " breathes a fireman. "This climb is going to have
to last you a long time!" "Crazy," answers a police voice.
"It's alright saving the ones who want to be saved:
it's the clowns who don't that make us into coppers —"
          By now the climber is not just a figure;
he has a face. "He's holding his breath!" cries someone.
Here the man reaches an iron grillework that leads
diagonally to the ground. Many run to haul him down,
then their arms drop, irresolute. Because he has upended
smoothly, as if underwater, and is descending
as if down cable into abyssal pressures.
You could swear bubbles streamed towards the ocean roof.
          By pure muscle power he comes down
grip after grip; his jeaned legs hang loosely upward;

even his hair seems to float. Photographers, shoaling,
fire stellar phosphorescences at him
                    and when he somersaults
at last to the ground, it is with levitatory slowness
and as he sprawls, dust and his limbs whirl up
and there is agony in his now goggling eyes
as half-awed officials carry him, feet trailing
through the eddying audience, seat him in a car and click
a belt across him, as if against an unexhausted buoyancy.

Writer in Residence
(or: Drop One of Your Own)

I was good at the Common Room game
but when Dr X dropped a name
it hung in the air
like a parachute flare
far over my head, to my shame.

A Public Figure

To break the Judaeo-Christian mould was his caper
but the ethic he served torched him with its newspaper.

The Young Woman Visitor

I never heard such boasting.
For two whole days while I was there
he never let up. He was the best axeman,
driver, horsebreaker, farmer, bullocky and judge
of standing timber "that ever God put guts in".
He'd also had the best dog, the best car,
the best crop of corn and the very best eight-day clock
and he'd been the best psalm-singer in his church, too.
Someone had let a little boy grow old;
I saw that all these things were a posy of flowers
snatched out of a funeral wreath and offered
to me, or to anyone,
not a wreath that would lie heaped on his grave
but the little special one that would go down
diminishing past clay, and trembling, on his coffin.

The Grandmother's Story

Just a few times in your life, you speak
those strange words. Or they speak themselves
out of you, before you can bite your tongue.
They are there, like a dream. You're not sure you've spoken
but you see them hit the other person
like a stone into floodwater. No splash much
but they go right to the bottom. To the soul.
No use saying you're sorry, or didn't mean them.

I never liked Ted Quarrie. Partly the way
he treated women. More, and it's the same,
the way he made poor Annie behave like him,
drinking and dribbling with Harold's whisky friends,
falling on the floor. The way they drank it:
Heere's luck! and pitch it down like castor oil;
they almost held their noses. They were like that at the show
when Ted sneaked up and pinched me. Hard, to hurt

and I hit him. Not slapped him. Shut my fist
and flattened him, in front of the whole showground.
I'd lumped more iron camp ovens, butter churns, and logs too
than ever he had. He stayed out for minutes.
When he came around, he cursed me. Called me every kind
of low-bred bitch. That's when I said — that other.
What did I say? That doesn't matter. I silenced him.
It would be a sin to do on purpose. To practise.

He hated me, ever after. And he hung round home
so I'd see him and know. But I've got a strong back;
I could bear it. You could still buy revolvers then
and he had one. But it took him years to creep away
round the verandahs, one Sunday, from where they were drinking
and lean in at our window, where I lay sick in bed.
He opened his coat, took out that thieves' gun, said
See this, Emily? It's for you. Poor thing. I nearly laughed.

Of course, I might have been shot for that. So I had to
look frightened, when really I was sick and tired
of the whole silliness. He went away, but my third boy
heard him, and followed. He was only seventeen
and Ted was a grown man. But he made him hand over
that gun in front of everyone. Harold never spoke, as usual.
The boys climbed up and dropped the thing down inside
the walling of this kitchen. It's still rusting there, I fancy.

The Line

Opium and vitriol and a plug of twist
added to the rum have left the Tiger prostrate,
snoring on his stripes in the sun.
                    Mickeen and Hoojah
step gingerly around him. Their own headache-bones
wince at the long saw's bare-fanged undulant clangour.

At the palace of a felled tree's crown, they strike up a fire,
share a pannikin of tea, then mix burnt bark with the dregs
and immerse a string in it.
                    Hold your end, Mickeen!
They walk either side of the sawdust-mealy pit
and pass the string above a chocked log. Precisely as Mercator

the wet black twine hovers half an inch above
the timber's knocked continents, tautens, is minutely
aligned. Then Hoojah plucks it.
                    The whipped note lays the first
straight line of a city, the first rectilinear thought
realised on that landscape. And marks it for division.

*Down in the hole, now. Sheeus late, a Vickeen!**
And keep yer feet on the ground, ye Fenyan bolter!
The black blade angles down,
                    is gripped: a rhythmic chaff
starts modelling sweat, choking ripe Donegal curses.
As each plank slats off, the saw sings its future as cattlebells.

The line has been printed six times, when the Tiger stumbles
across from their tent with bread and three pounds of salt beef
stuck on a bayonet.
                    At least it's not the poisonous snake
he slung into the pit last time the rum clawed at him.
Belching after a feed, he rips the handles downward

as if to pull the merciful saw through himself
or drag work itself down on his anguish, like Samson.
Don't jerk a woman
                    right though the cut, there, Tiger!
Shouts Hoojah, laughing, *or I'll be narrer and flat.*
Taste, reverence and polemic close over the gang after that.

* Down with you, Micky! (Anglicised Irish)

Mercurial September

Preindustrial haze. The white sky rim
forecasts a hot summer. Burning days
indeed are rehearsed, with flies and dinnertime fan
but die out, over west mountains
erased with azure, into spring-cool nights
and the first flying insects
which are the small weeds of a bedroom window.

Early in the month, the valley was a Friesian cow:
knobbed black, whitened straw.
Alarming smokes bellied up behind the heights of forest.
Now green has invested fires'
fixed cloud-shadows; lower gum boughs are seared chestnut.
Emerald kingparrots, crimson-breasted, whirr
and plane out of open feed sheds.

Winds are changeable. We're tacking.
West on rubbed blue days,
easterlies on hot, southerly and dead calm for rain.
Mercury is near the moon, Venus at perigee
and frogs wind their watches all night on swampy stretches
where waterhens blink with their white tails at dusk, like rabbits,
and the mother duck does her cripple act.

Dams glitter like house roofs again.
The first wasp comes looking for a spider to paralyse:
a flimsy ultralight flier
who looks like a pushover, but after one pass lifts
you, numb, out of your trampoline. Leaves together
as for prayer or diving, bean plants erupt
into the grazing glory. Those unnibbled spread their arms.

Poddy calves wobbling in their newborn mushroom colours
ingest and make the pungent custard of infancy.
Sign of a good year, many snakes lie flattened
on the roads again. Bees and pollens drift
through greening orchards. And next day it pours rain:
smokes of cloud on every bushland slope,
that opposite, wintry haze. The month goes out facing backwards.

Extract from a Verse Letter to Dennis Haskell

Dear Dennis,
                    Warm thanks for your letter
in verse. It's very much better,
nicer and more thoughtful than those
postcards packed with minuscule prose
I write even to friends, like the harrassed
editor I once was. I'm impressed.
Moved, too, that you should miss my company
— I never quite expect that, perhaps funnily,
of people. Yes, too much ochre
separates us now, joker from joker.
It's a bore that the width of the continent
can't be secretly folded or bent
so's to let us yarn here on the crest
of Deer's Hill, watching sunsets on Rottnest,
or strolling, well fed, by the Swan
as it flows beside our vegie garden.
I think you'd like it here, in our glade
of fruit saplings that now nearly manage shade
and soft grass, beside the lotus dam
and our other trees. Some year you must see them.
Trees, space, waterbirds — things of that ilk,
plus people of my own kind, are the milk
and honey I came home for. Not dairying,
that drudgery, poor, imprisoning, unvarying.
At eighteen, I made a great vow
I'd never milk another bloody cow.
It was only after I won my battle
to be free of them, that I came to love cattle.
Few dairy here now, anyway. It's gone largely bung.
I'm forty eight next week. I won't die a dairyman. Or young.
The bush permits allusion, not illusion:
I didn't come for any past that's gone.
More for Dad, who had stopped getting on
and was getting old and sick. Our eldest children
too had already missed a country childhood
and we didn't think the younger three should
have to. Also there was this choice I had:
get out of Yuppie City or go mad.
No perhaps in that either. But enough.
Life here is scarcely tough:
Valerie's wryly and happily learning bush ways
and would have mastered the harder ones, too, of the old days.
She's on leave from teaching. Alec goes to special school by bus,

Clare to a local school. I'm running my export business
out of this room from which, well, four bean rows
and two of turnips are visible. Peter, our smallest boy
is enjoying his babyhood, but sometimes gets wistful for Sydney.
Dad's had a cataract op. and sees well for his age
but now he's got shingles, nailed not to rafters but his rib-cage.
Ouch! Still, spring here delivers days you could dance to,
given a chance to. And that is our news.

Max Fabre's Yachts*

Towers of swell fabric
leaning on the ocean
go about in salt haze
to race for the rocked gun.

Straining theory makes the world
equivocal as miracles
ever were. Between spear and sphere
here tussle in purified war

the souls of rich men,
of syndicates and winch-winders
but no longer do they skate
on a sunk ice of ambition.

Nothing turns on a blade: all
now glide on a lucky trefoil,
a trinitarian trifoil,
vision of a drowning man

and first unveiled off Newport:
Hermes, messenger of Heaven
speeding with one winged foot
dipped in the ocean.

* Max Fabre, of Sydney, made pioneering designs in the early 1960s of trifoil
"winged" keel forms for ocean racing yachts.

Freshwater and Salt

It's the opening of the surf season
thirty miles away east;
most things speak a different dialect
over there on the coast.

Here, the rising wave comes as
grass. The animals drink it
thirstily. It's a sweetwater ocean.
If your house is fenced in, it'll sink it.

Fire and snakes swim in it;
you have to slash and mow.
Time for rotary blades, and weeping salt water
with your whole skin as you make them go.

It isn't in fact such a whelming
tide. But it's an ever-swelling one
you have to keep in balance, like the Dutch.
Much worse when it doesn't run

and even the cities are stranded
by the fresh sea they're really built on,
the shark-free, drown-you-quick, money-devious
child not of moons but the sun.

I'm delighted how the world's widest ocean
can hide under other names: the air,
ice sheets, ink, farming history. But life's saline
skins and linings are its ultimate shore.

Between us here and the breakers
there's that salt rind of chip-frying city
twelve thousand miles long, that locals
will come home from soon with gritty

trunksfull and running shoes full
of ground bottle, ground coral, ground shell.
I guess we're all flesh of that shell
and will broach it by New Year, and wade gingerly

up to our nacres in salt swirl,
even we freshwater pearlers
and privately pale herbage hurlers
happiest on the grassed forms of groundswell.

The Australia Card

Hey True Blue, they are slipping one to you:
don't you feel the dimensions?
They are sliding in a card — pushing smoothly but not hard —
between you and your pretensions.

Their pretext is dole bludgers, those half-fictional sub-drudges
who multiply peanuts by three,
and in a time of slump, they must drain that vital sump
they call the Black Economy.

They guessed they could depend, Blue, on your meanness in the end, Blue
to insinuate a burglar's slip of plastic
between you and your rights, Blue. "It's a spunky pair of tights, Blue,
with your own portrait on the elastic!"

Well you have or claim more rights than a dingo pup has bites,
more rights than any brumby in the yard,
but Bluey that's all wrong, for your "rights" will soon belong
not to you but to that little plastic card,

to the microchips that make it and the stone-faced goons who'll take it,
"Just checking, sir or madam. Ah! A Jew!"
(There are some who might alarm you on just how IDs can harm you
but they speak a funny accent, don't they, Blue?)

Your rights, if you pursue them, will be kept for you to view them
briefly, like your income at the bank:
show your card, go up the stair, have it checked by those up there
and a slot will print your life out on a blank.

If you cry that isn't you they will shrug "Prove it, True Blue."
If it's you but wrong that will be just as hard —
"In the meantime we'll arrest you: we have flash fines to divest you
of what's mucking up the data on your card!"

"If you've nothing on your conscience" — any dero could shout Nonshense!
Black folk could tell you how it used to feel
to be licensed like a dog just to keep your kids, drink grog,
cash a cheque or vote, but never be quite real.

Where's your protests now, my treasure, at or even in this measure?
(What's the drum, Red Gum? Ho hum?)
Are your sunlit brains extended, just to see this menace ended?
Do the people live for government's sake? (strum strum).

Or is government for the people? Or as you've mostly done
will you weakly let that slide and try to cheat them?
Kids, your apathy's no use, and your strutting's self-abuse:
every time, you know, most of you fail to beat them.

Hey True Blue, they are slipping it to you,
they'll do it in the end in all positions.
They are sliding in a card, while you are off your guard,
between you and your traditions.

Must we conclude that you are descended from a screw
as much as from the lags he had to guard?
What would proud Ben Hall say? Or the Digs who gave their all, say?
Would they reckon that the bronze had turned to lard?
Or merely sigh that failure
was the first rhyme for Australia
and there'll soon be no Australia? Just a slick Australia Card.

The Man with the Hoe

Thinking about air conditioning's Willis Carrier
who also won the West, I am turning
earth in on a long potato drill,
which is like folding history down on trench lines

of unnumbered mild faces. The day
is overcast, with rain pricking the air
and us to hurry, plying our hoes along this promontory
above Horses Creek. The channel-billed cuckoo

shouts, flying, and the drug squad helicopter
comes singing *I'll spot it, your pot plot.*
O lord of love, look from above
sang the churches, but what looks down

from beyond the sky now's the television
of a spy satellite, feeding the coordinates
of today's cloud nations into spinning
tapes for the updating screens of judgement.

The Lord of love is in decay. Relievedly.
He's in worn flanks of stonework, in weathering
garden posts, in the survival of horses,
in humans' long survival after mating, in ticky tacky

buildings that mean the builders were paid properly
and not always by magnates. He is more apparent
in the idea, verandahs and visitings of a hospital
than the stunning theatre. More in surrounds than the centre

where he is ground against, love versus love, he lives
in the bantering pauses. The pattern of love's also
behind our continuing to cover these potatoes
which, by her mercy, also look like potatoes.

Warmth makes cool. The mystery of refrigeration —
but now three fighter aircraft distil out
of the north hills, fast, ahead of their enormous
collapse of sound. Cloud resorbs them. As in the bra ad

the heart lifts and separates, shrivelled with exultation
that is the angel of history: a boy bored rigid
with farmwork sights along a noble light-draining
sword blade held at the level of his mouth.

Cold. Burning cold. The old tremendous imagery
of the Judgement recycles cold, in a bitter age
where love is passion, and passion is the action.
Who could trust a God of love, now we have seen

the love that ignites stars, and ourselves possess such ignition?
Who would trust a god on heat nearer than the stars?
Who can trust heat, that may now freeze the planet?
Who can trust coldness, matrix of utter heat?

We cry for cool, because we long for warmth.
When the fighters grow obsolete, and their pipes cool,
warmth reinvests them. It seems a reversing cycle.
Let the Lord be warm and cool, and judgement be

a flower I'm not good enough to unfold yet,
as I stitch down this earth, and my uncle comes driving
his skittish young tractor over our holey paddock,
my uncle the ex-smoker — not pot: we're older than the pot lot —

who starts conversations with a ruminative ahaanh,
not *aha! I've caught you!* A shyer reconnecting ahaanh
warm from past meetings. This is among my people
whom I do understand, but not before they speak.

The Misery Cord

Misericord. The Misery Cord.
It was lettered on a wall.
I knew that cord, how it's tough to break
however hard you haul.

My cousin sharefarmed, and so got half:
half dignity, half hope, half income,
for his full work. To get a place
of his own took his whole lifetime.

Some pluck the misery chord from habit
or for luck, whatever they feel,
some to deceive, and some for the tune —
but sometimes it's real.

Milking bails, flannel shirts, fried breakfasts,
these were our element,
and doubling on horses, and shouting Score!
at a dog yelping on a hot scent,

but an ambulance racing on our back road
is bad news for us all:
the house of community is about
to lose a plank from its wall.

Grief is nothing you can do, but do;
worst work for least reward,
pulling your heart out through both eyes
with tugs of the misery cord.

I looked at my cousin's farm, where he'd just
built his family a house of their own,
and I looked down into Fred's next house,
its clay walls of bluish maroon.

Just one man has snapped the misery cord
and lived. He said once was enough.
A poem is an afterlife on earth:
Christ grant us the other half.

Infant among Cattle

Young parents, up at dawn, working. Their first child can't
be his own babysitter, so as they machine the orphaned milk
from their cows, he must sit plump on the dairy cement,
the back of his keyhole pants safetypinned to a stocking

that is tied to a bench leg. He studies a splotch of cream,
how the bubbles in it, too thick to break, work like
the coated and lucid gravels in the floor. On which he then dings
a steel thing, for the tingling in it and his fingers

till it skips beyond his tether. As the milkers front up
in their heel-less skiddy shoes, he hangs out aslant
on his static line, watching the breeching rope brace them
and their washed udders relieved of the bloodberry ticks

that pull off a stain, and show a calyx of kicking filaments.
By now the light stands up behind the trees like sheet iron.
It photographs the cowyard and dairy-and-bails in one vast
buttery shadow wheel on the trampled junction of paddocks

where the soil is itself a concrete, of dust and seedy stones
and manure crustings. When his father slings a bucketful
of wash water out the door, it wallops and skids
and is gulped down by a sudden maw like the cloth of a radio.

Out and on out, the earth tightens down on the earth
and squeezes heat up through the yellowing grass
like a surfaceless fluid, to pool on open country,
to drip from faces, and breed the insect gleams of midday.

Under the bench, crooning this without words to his rag dog,
he hears a vague trotting outside increase — and the bull
erupts, aghast, through the doorway, dribbling, clay in his curls,
a slit orange tongue working in and out under his belly —

and is repulsed, with buckets and screams and a shovel.
The little boy, swept up in his parents' distress, howls then
but not in fear of the bull, who seemed a sad apparition:
a huge prostrate man, bewildered by a pitiless urgency.

Variations on a Measure of Burns

When January is home to visit her folks
and official work is a public hoax,
soy sprouts dotting the serpentine strokes
      ploughs combed in the lacquered
hill soil that each afternoon's rainstorm soaks
      weave a green jacquard

and zucchini and wart squash and Queensland Blues
(not the dog, but the pumpkin) squeak together like shoes
in tractor trailers, and nectarines bruise
      from being awaited,
but the grizzled haze over mountain views
      looks faintly methylated

because Drought, who's in on every forced sale,
though he may have seen the farmers granted bail
this summer, has the continent in his entail.
      Even smashed, he's seen you:
that old man up a back road fumbling his mail
      gets letters from El Niño.

Disappointment, holiday and heatwave shilly-shally
round this snaky time of year. Stock prices plunge and rally
but the government's retreated for keeps from this valley:
      the flash brick erstwhile
Whitlam toilet block lacks its school, and stands orphaned on its gulley;
      the PO's a closed file.

We retain a public phone and some dirt main roads
on whose corners part-time squatters tip sprawling loads
of gravel for drunk drivers who for lifetimes and by codes
      like Whoa car! and hug-the-crown
miraculously get home to treat their families like toads
      or finish upside down

      in the dark, miles from town,
standing on my scalp with the rain's sparks falling upward,
      windscreen a collective noun,
delighted by the spinning tyre slowing above the cupboard
and the glare-path through inverted trees — myself as I could
have been, through brutal labour for a bare livelihood,

        myself on that quest
few families dare acknowledge, let alone go with you on,
        the hunger for the Rest
when mortgage world time politics, everything's on top of one
and the teenage girl you married is not months but decades gone:
I'm sorry for myself in his sideburns and cardigan.

        O he will like that,
murmurs his wife, wrestling farm accounts, steering above the rocks,
then bundling the children off to bed, switching off the box:
        Television makes you fat!
Our concern cuts away at once. Moorhen and flying fox
outside creak identical rusty keys in their vocal locks
        and the dark stands pat.

Aspects of Language and War on the Gloucester Road

I travel a road cut through time
by bare feet and boots without socks,
by eight-year-old men droving cattle,
by wheels parallel as printed rhyme
over rhythms of hill shale and tussocks.
> In the hardest real trouble of my life
> I called this Gloucester road to mind,
> which cuttings were bare gravel, which rife
> with grass, which ones rainforest-vined.
The road starts at Coolongolook
which means roughly Leftward Inland
from *gulunggal,* the left hand,
runs west between Holdens' and James'
where new people have to paint names
on their mailboxes, and stumps have board-slots
from when tall trees were jibbed like yachts
and felled above their hollow tones.
Later logs lie about like gnawed bones.
The road comes on through Sawyers Creek
where the high whaleback ridge becomes a peak
and where my father, aged nine years
faced down the Bashing Teacher, a Squeers
who cut six-foot canes in the scrub
and, chewing his tongue in a sub-
jective ecstasy, lashed back-arching children.
Mind your mhisness! — Time someone chipped you! —
Short blazed at tall — and the knobbed cane withdrew.
My father was cheered shoulder-high in the playground then
and the flogging rods vanished. But previously slack
parents loomed, shouting. And behind them, the sack.
> Here too a farmer heard *Give up*
> *cigarettes or your life!* He coughed a sup
> of Flanders gas, cried *Jesus Christ and that,*
> *Doctor, I'll give up my life!* And what
> was burning inside him smouldered on
> for decades, disclosed only once
> in '39, teaching dodges to his sons.
> (*1939,* smiles an aunt, *the year*
> *when no woman had to stay a spinster.*)
The road runs through Bunyah, meaning bark
for shelters, or firelighters' candlebark
blown on in a *gugri* house, a word
for fire-hut that is still heard
though few farms still use a googery.

Few? None now. I was gone a generation.
Even parrot-eating's stopped: — *The buggers,*
they'd been eating that wild-tobacco berry:
Imagine a soup of boiled cigars! —
        I'm driving to Gloucester station
        to collect my urban eldest from the train,
        and there are the concrete tips
        of bridge piles, set like a tank trap
        up a farm entryway. The huge rap
        of a piledriver shivered few chips
        off the bedrock when they were banged stubbornly
        by an engineer who would not be told
        black rock at eight feet'll stop you cold!
        what did locals know, lacking a degree?
        I loved the old bridge, its handrails,
        ballast logs and deck, an inland ship.
        Kids watched how floods' pewter rip
        wracked limbs over it. Floods were our folktales.
        Now we drive above missed schooldays, high
        on the Shire's concrete second try.
There at the hall, drums and accordions
still pump, and well-lit dancers glide.
In the dark outside move, single and duo,
the angrily shy and the bawdy ones:
blood and babies from the dancing outside.
        We held Free Church services too, though,
        in that hall. For months I'd cry aloud
        at the rise in the east of any cloud
        no bigger than a man's hand.
        A cloud by day led me out of Babyland
        about when Hiroshima had three years to go.
The Free Church, knuckle-white on its ridge
now looks north at the Lavinia Murray Bridge,
at my great-grandmother's Chinese elm tree
and the Dutchman tractoring peaceably.
That faint scar across the creek is butts
of a range for aligned wartime rifle shots.
        What fearsome breach of military law
        sent you, Lieutenant Squance, to command
        that platoon of worried men-on-the-land
        the Bunyah Volunteer Defence Corps
        in those collapsing months after Singapore,
        brassbuttoned fathers, deadly afraid
        for life and family? Your British parade
        manner gave them some diversion:
        milky boots, casual mutiny, aspersion,
        your corporal raving death-threats in your face
        for calling his clean rifle a disgrace,
        brownpaper sandwiches sent to you with tea
        after parade one Saturday —

I think, though, you'd have stayed and defended
us, and died as our world ended,
Mr Squance. Belated thanks are extended.
There's a house where I had hospitality
without fuss for years when I needed it.
Now it's dying, of sun-bleach, of shadowed
scarlet lichen, the poisons of abandonment.
I'm thinking, over the next rises,
of children who did not have their lives,
who died young, and how one realises
only at home that, unknown to younger wives,
faces lie in wait in finger-felted albums'
gapless groupings of family. The sums
of those short lifetimes add to one's own age,
to its weight, having no light yarns to lift them.
Peace or war, all die for our freedom.
The innocent, the guilty, the beasts, all die for our freedom.
I was taught the irreparable knowledge
by a baby of thirty next door in his wheelchair
who'd thrash and grimace with happiness when I went there.
I see the road, and many roads before
through a fawn snap of him as a solemn little boy
before meningitis. And it is first for him
that I insist on a state where lives resume.

      The squatter style grinds eastward here, or 'down'
      (both *ba:rung* in the old language) and spreads out from town.
      One property here was Something Downs for a bit:
      over there through the hills I can glimpse part of it
      just short of the pines round my gone one-teacher school
      with its zigzag air raid trench and morning flagpole;
      from there I remember birthdays, and how to shin
      fast over fence rails: *You're last! — I'll be first in Heaven!*
      I pass by Lavinia's gate,
      the first woman Shire President in the State
      and not dowager at eighty, but reigning, in her fox fur,
      descending on Parliament, ascending with the cropduster
      whose rent for an airfield was shopping flights to Gloucester.
A flagman stops me with a circled word.
I halt beside him, wait till he can be heard
over a big steel roller's matt declensions
as it tightens gravel down into two dimensions.
He points at a possum curled like an ampersand
around a high dead branch, spending the day
miserably where its light caught her away
from her cache of darkness. — *There's her baby's hand*
out of her pouch. — She's dreaming. — Wonder if we
are in her dream? — Wonder if she's ever seen a hill? —
What lights would we have, on what cars, if we were nocturnal?
Look lower, native bees. — Round a knothole spout

a thought-balloon of grist breathes in and out.
Look, one on your arm. — Their mixture must need salt.
Hell will have icecream before this road gets asphalt.
      I drive off, on what sounds like a shore.
      In Upper Bunyah there are more
      settlers without nicknames, or
      none they know. The widower on that hill
      used to have one (and he was the raving corporal).
      He once had some evangelists staying
      in his house, demonstratively praying,
      so one day his two dozen cats annoyed him
      and he took the small rifle and destroyed them,
      shot them off rafters, sniped eyes under his bed —
      cups exploded in the kitchen as poor Tibby fled —
      the men of prayer too ran headlong from his charity.
      Sweet, for one, are the uses of barbarity.
His later wife had a chequebook and painted in France.
why does so much of our culture work through yarns
equivalent to the national talent for cartoons?
It is an old war brought from Europe
by those who also brought poverty and landscape.
They had scores to settle, even with themselves. Tradition
is also repeating oneself, expecting inattention,
singing dumb, expecting scorn. Or sly mispronunciation
out of loyalty to the dead: *You boiling them bikinis*
in that Vichy sauce? We were the wrong people risen
— forerunners in that of nearly everyone —
but we rose early, on small farms, and were family.
A hard yarn twangs the tension
and fires its broad arrow out of a grim space
of Old Australian smells: toejam, tomato sauce,
semen and dead singlets the solitary have called peace
but which is really an unsurrendered trench. Really prison.
      It is a reminder all stories are of war.
      Peace, and the proof of peace, is the verandah
      absent from some of the newer houses here.
      It is also a slight distance — as indeed
      grows between me and the farm of my cousin
      who recently was sold treated seed grain
      in mistake for cattle-feed grain:
      it killed cows, but he dared not complain
      or sue the feed merchant, for fear
      he'd be barred as a milk supplier
      to the Milk Board, and ruined, and in consequence
      see his house become somebody's rural residence.
      Such things can make a farmer look down, at his land
      between his boots, and dignity shrink in his hand.
Now the road enters the gesture of the hills
where they express geologic weather

and contend with landscape in spills
of triangular forest down fence lines
and horse-and-scoop dams like filled mines.
What else to say of peace? It is a presence
with the feeling of home, and timeless in any tense.
   I am driving *waga,* up and west.
   Parting cattle, I climb over the crest
   out of Bunyah, and skirt Bucca Wauka,
   A Man Sitting Up With Knees Against His Chest:
   baga waga, knees up, the burial-shape of a warrior.
Eagles flying below me, I will ascend Wallanbah,
that whipcrack country of white cedar
and ruined tennis courts, and speed up on the tar.
In sight of the high ranges I'll pass the turnoff to Bundook,
Hindi for musket — which it also took
to add to the daylight species here, in the prim-
al 1830s of our numbered Dreamtime
   and under the purple coast of the Mograni
   and its trachyte west wall scaling in the sky
   I will swoop to the valley and Gloucester Rail
   where boys hand-shunted trains to load their cattle
   and walk on the platform, glancing west at that country
   or running creeks, the stormcloud-coloured Barrington,
   the land, in lost Gaelic and Kattangal, of Barandan.